# DIPLOMATIC HANDBOOK

Sixth Edition

## R. G. Feltham

Sometime Sub-Warden of Queen Elizabeth House and
Director, Oxford University Foreign Service Programme

LONGMAN
London and New York

**Longman Group UK Limited,**
Longman House, Burnt Mill,
Harlow, Essex CM20 2JE, England
*and Associated Companies throughout the world.*

*Published in the United States of America*
*by Longman Publishing, New York*

First published 1970
Second edition 1977
Third edition 1980
Fourth edition 1982
Fifth edition 1988
Sixth edition 1992

ISBN 0 582 099528 PPR

**British Library Cataloguing-in-Publication Data**

A catalogue record for this book is
available from the British Library

**Library of Congress Cataloging-in-Publication Data**

Feltham, R. G. (Ralph George)
    Diplomatic handbook / R.G. Feltham. – 6th ed.
        p.   cm.
    Includes index.
    ISBN 0–582–09952–8
    1. Diplomatic and consular service.   2. United Nations.
I. Title.
JX1662.F4   1993
341.3′3 – dc20
                                                93–15074
                                                CIP

Set by 5 in 10/11 Times Roman

Printed in Malaysia by PMS

# CONTENTS

# Contents

# PREFACE

The aim of this book is to provide a concise but comprehensive source of relevant information for those who are embarking on an international and, particularly, a diplomatic career.

It has been revised with the assistance of diplomats from many countries and members of international organisations, to all of whom I am deeply indebted for their unfailing courtesy and assistance.

I would like to express my particular appreciation to my colleagues at the Netherlands Institute of International Relations 'Clingendael'; Henriette Feltham-van Dijk, Deputy-Head of the Netherlands Embassy Bureau in Berlin, Dato' A. S. Talalla Director-General of the Malaysian Institute of Diplomacy and Foreign Relations, and Alison Nicol administrator of the Oxford University Foreign Service Programme; and above all to those whom I have had the privilege of teaching over the past twenty-five years: they have provided inspiration, enthusiasm and good fellowship, and I am the richer for their company.

I would also like to take this opportunity to point out that the word 'diplomat' in the English language can have either a masculine or feminine connotation, and if at any point in the text it is followed by the masculine personal pronoun it is solely to avoid the tedium of 'he or she': it is not intended to have any other significance.

*Berlin*                                                              *R.G.F.*

# ACKNOWLEDGEMENTS

We are indebted to the following for permission to reproduce copyright material:

Council of Europe for various extracts from *The European Extradition Convention* by the Council of Europe; the author for an appendix from *Dictionary of Economic Terms* by A. Gilpin; the Controller of Her Majesty's Stationery Office for extracts from *Treaty Series Command Papers* and A. W. Sijthoff International Publishing Co. for an extract from *Conference Diplomacy* by J. Kaufmann.

*Chapter 1*

# DIPLOMATIC RELATIONS

## INTRODUCTION

At the present stage of man's development his world is divided into over 180 units called states. How and why the states came to have the shape and population they have today is mainly a matter of historical accident and personal design. Within a state the rule of law prevails, and those who break the law are punished. But outside the territory of a state no such law exists, and the choice between international anarchy and international harmony rests freely with the individual states. Towards fellow-states they may behave responsibly or irresponsibly, peacefully or aggressively; even a negative, isolationist attitude can be beneficial or harmful, for every state is a member of a community and not only its action but also its inaction affects the whole.

The main objective of any state in its relations with other states is to direct and influence these relations for its own maximum advantage; but at the same time, and if only in self-interest, it has the responsibility of formulating its policies towards other states and managing its relations in the interests of world harmony, thus helping to prevent wars and the waste of wealth. The formulation of foreign policy is one of the aspects of national politics and is the task of the politician, while the management of international relations and the reconciliation of diverse foreign policy priorities is the task of the diplomat.

The basis of diplomacy is communication – of thoughts and ideas – between the governments of states (and to an increasing extent with international organisations), and this can be effected directly between heads of government or indirectly through the intermediary of written correspondence or of an ambassador. Between the super-states and between neighbouring states diplomacy at its highest

1

level can most easily and most logically be conducted by heads of government meeting together face to face and exchanging their thoughts and ideas – talking, reasoning and discussing; but, because of their variety and complexity, diplomatic relations in general can only be conducted indirectly, and centuries of experience have shown that the person of an ambassador is indispensable for this purpose. But an ambassador rarely works on his own: he is the head of a diplomatic mission which, working together as a team, provides the basic and all-important link between government and government or between government and international organisation.

Moreover, since the breaching of the Berlin Wall in 1989 which symbolically marked the end of Tsarist and Communist imperial rule in Europe and Asia and, for the past forty-five years, the attempt of the Soviet Union to maintain a military presence and political influence worldwide, the role of the diplomat has taken on a new dimension.

If history is any guide, the collapse of the Soviet empire will result in social and political consequences as fundamental and as far-reaching as those that followed the dissolution of earlier empires, whether Napoleonic, Ottoman, Austro-Hungarian or British: the major difference being the suddenness and extent of the collapse, and the total unpreparedness of governments for such an eventuality.

In Europe, for as long as most people can remember, NATO and the European Community together with Comecon and the Warsaw Pact provided the framework within which states operated. Now Comecon and the Warsaw Pact have been disbanded, NATO has lost its front line and perceived *raison d'être* (except as a visible assurance of continuing American concern); whilst the twelve countries of the Community which could, with some legitimacy, claim to represent 'Europe' when only the West had freedom of choice, now find that all the countries of Europe – over fifty of them – are seeking to regain their European heritage.

In every corner of the world, the end of super-power confrontation raises problems and offers opportunities, and requires every country to review and re-define its foreign policy priorities. We are living through an avalanche of history, and it is no exaggeration to say that the world is entering a phase of change and uncertainty in its international relations unparalleled in recorded history.

For diplomats, the coming years are bound to be a period of intense and increasing activity. For half a century, they were only able to operate within the constraints imposed by the military. For forty-five years the Cold War was prevented from turning into a real war by the two adversaries maintaining the balance of their forces in equilibrium rather than – as in former times – by diplomats. They will, however, be operating in a very different environment and will need to acquire a more critical, more analytical, more constructive attitude towards the problems that the present upheaval will inevitably produce, and to re-learn the old diplomatic skills. They will also have to understand a new factor: the impact of the current 'Media Revolution' on the formulation of foreign policy, on the methods of diplomacy and on political activity – the advent of global political awareness: it is a revolution as profound and as significant as was Gutenberg's invention of moveable metal type, and will result in social and political consequences of comparable magnitude.

We are living at a time when the Old World Order has collapsed and a New World Order is nowhere in sight: our only hope lies in the successful conduct of diplomatic relations.

# THE ESTABLISHMENT OF DIPLOMATIC RELATIONS AND OF PERMANENT DIPLOMATIC MISSIONS

## GENERAL PRINCIPLES AND PURPOSES

Diplomatic relations between states may be established by friendly contacts of any form between their governments; but permanent diplomatic relations are considered to exist only with the establishment of a diplomatic mission, or preferably with the exchange of diplomatic missions. These are established by mutual consent and on the basis of a mutual understanding of the functions that will be undertaken by the mission. These functions have become generally accepted over past centuries, and have been defined in the 1961 Vienna Convention on Diplomatic Relations as consisting, basically, of:

(a) representing the sending state in the receiving state;
(b) protecting in the receiving state the interests of the sending state and its nationals, within the limits permitted by international law;
(c) negotiating with the government of the receiving state;
(d) ascertaining, by all lawful means, conditions and developments in the receiving state, and reporting thereon to the government of the sending state;
(e) promoting friendly relations between the sending state and the receiving state, and developing their economic cultural and scientific relations.

Apart from their diplomatic functions, members of the diplomatic staff of a mission may also act in a consular capacity.

3

## CLASSES OF HEADS OF MISSION

Heads of mission may be of one of three classes depending on the mutual agreement of the governments concerned:

1. Ambassadors, Apostolic Nuncios or Pro-Nuncios, and other heads of mission of equivalent rank (e.g. High Commissioners exchanged between Commonwealth countries) who are accredited to Heads of State.
2. Envoys, Ministers and Papal Internuncios who are accredited to Heads of State. (This class is now virtually non-existent).
3. Chargés d'Affaires (*en titre*, *en pied*, or titular) who are accredited to Ministers for Foreign Affairs.

No differentiation may be made between heads of mission on account of their class, except in matters of precedence and protocol, and in that the right of access to a Head of State is normally reserved to those of ambassadorial rank.

## TITLES OF HEADS OF MISSION

It is usual for an Ambassador to be styled 'Ambassador Extraordinary and Plenipotentiary'. (An Ambassador Extraordinary and Plenipotentiary was at one time superior in status to a resident Ambassador.) Similarly the head of a legation is likely to be styled 'Envoy Extraordinary and Minister Plenipotentiary'.

## APPROVAL OF A HEAD OF MISSION BY THE HOST STATE

Before a head of mission is appointed to a post, the approval or *agrément* of the receiving state is sought confidentially. This approval will normally be given, but may be withheld if it is considered that the person concerned is not acceptable and in this event no reason has to be given. In practice, an official hint of unacceptability would normally be enough for a nomination to be withdrawn.

## CREDENTIALS

A head of mission is provided with credentials to prove his authenticity to the Head of State to which he is accredited. These are alternatively referred to as Letters of Credence and are somewhat ornate in style, e.g.

*For Ambassadors*

To [full name and title of head of state]

Excellency:
I have appointed X.Y.Z., a distinguished citizen of [name of sending state], to represent me before your Government as Ambassador Extraordinary and Plenipotentiary of [name of sending state].

He is well aware of the mutual interests of our two countries and shares my sincere desire to preserve and enhance the long friendship between us.

My faith in his high character and ability gives me entire confidence that he will carry out his duties in a manner fully acceptable to you.

Accordingly I entrust him to your confidence. I ask that you receive him favourably, and give full credence to what he shall say on the part of [name of sending state] as well as to the assurances which he bears of my best wishes for the prosperity of [name of receiving state].

Yours very truly

[Signature of Head of State]

By the head of state

[Signature of Minister of Foreign Affairs]

[Place]          [Date]

In the Commonwealth the Sovereign is Head of eighteen of the fifty-one (formerly British) member states, and when heads of mission are exchanged between such states they are provided with a *letter of introduction* from Prime Minister to Prime Minister.

When a Head of State who is a sovereign dies or otherwise ceases to reign, the credentials of all heads of mission accredited to the sovereign become invalid; similarly the credentials issued by the sovereign become invalid, and in both instances require renewal. This requirement does not, however, apply in the event of the death of a President or the termination of his period of office, and is no longer effective in the kingdoms of Denmark, Sweden and the Netherlands.

## DATE OF ASSUMPTION OF FUNCTIONS

A head of mission of ambassadorial rank is considered to have taken up his functions in the state to which he is accredited when he has presented his credentials to the Head of State. In a few states (notably the UK) he is considered to have taken up functions when he has notified the appropriate ministry (usually the Ministry of Foreign Affairs) of his arrival and has presented them with a working copy (*copie d'usage*) of his credentials. The ceremonies for the formal acceptance of heads of mission are held strictly in the order that they arrived to take up their functions.

## NATIONALITY OF A HEAD OF MISSION

A head of mission will, save in most exceptional circumstances, have the nationality of the state he is representing; but this requirement does not necessarily apply to his spouse. In many diplomatic services officers may be given special permission to marry foreign nationals provided the circumstances and the particular nationality involved are such that they do not in any way jeopardise or interfere with the officer's career. In Arab countries it is the general rule that diplomats may not marry foreigners, though in certain instances the Head of State may authorise marriage to other Arabs.

## NATIONALITY OF MEMBERS OF THE DIPLOMATIC STAFF

The members of the diplomatic staff of a mission should in principle be nationals of the state they serve, but in exceptional cases they may be nationals of the state in which the mission is situated; in this event, the specific approval of the host state must be obtained, and it may be withdrawn at any time.

## ACCREDITATION TO MORE THAN ONE STATE

A head of mission may be accredited (and members of the diplomatic staff assigned) to more than one state, provided there is no objection on the part of any of the states concerned. In the event of such an arrangement, Chargés d'Affaires *ad interim* (or in certain circumstances members of the diplomatic staff of lesser standing) may be established in diplomatic missions in those capitals where the head of mission does not have his permanent seat.

## INTERNATIONAL ORGANISATIONS: ACCREDITATION OF HEADS OF MISSION

A head of mission (or any member of the diplomatic staff of his mission) may act as representative of his state to any international organisation, and in this instance the state to which he is accredited need not be informed, nor may it raise any objection.

## THE SEAT OF A DIPLOMATIC MISSION

A diplomatic mission is established in the capital of a state; additional offices forming part of the mission may only be established in other parts of the state if special permission is given by that state. In a few instances, e.g. the Netherlands, the diplomatic capital is different from the capital of the country.

## THE SIZE OF A MISSION

The size of diplomatic missions may be agreed on a reciprocal basis; alternatively a state may require that the number of members of a mission should be kept within reasonable limits taking into consideration the circumstances and conditions in the host state and the needs of the mission. Within such limits, and provided that the principle of representation by its own nationals is adhered to, a state should be free to appoint whomsoever it wishes to any of its diplomatic missions. In the case of military, naval and air attachés it is within the discretion of the Ministry of Foreign Affairs to require their names to be submitted in advance, and for approval to be obtained before any appointment is made. A state may also refuse to accept officials of a particular category, provided that the restriction is applied on a non-discriminatory basis to all diplomatic missions in the state.

## ACCREDITATION BY MORE THAN ONE STATE

Two or more states may, in exceptional circumstances, accredit the same person as head of mission to another state, unless objection is raised by the receiving state.

## DECLARATION OF '*PERSONA NON GRATA*' OR '*NON-ACCEPTABLE*'

A state has the right to declare a head of a mission or member of his diplomatic staff to be unacceptable (*persona non grata*) and to inform his government accordingly. In this event the diplomat's functions are terminated and he is (unless a national or permanent resident of the state in which he is serving) recalled. If his government takes no such step, the host state may refuse to recognise him as being a member of the mission. The declaration of *persona non grata* may be made either before or after the diplomat's arrival, and no reasons for it have to be given.

Similarly, members of the administrative and technical staff may be declared *non-acceptable*.

There are two principal grounds on which a diplomat may be declared *persona non grata*: those which spring from personal weakness, and result in criminal or antisocial behaviour; and deliberate acts hostile to the security or other interests of the state, carried out under the cloak of diplomatic immunity. A further possible pretext for a diplomat being so declared is as a retaliation against a state that has declared one of its own diplomats to be *persona non grata*; but although such practice is contrary to the spirit of international relations, it is regrettably not infrequent.

### OBLIGATIONS ACCEPTED BY A HOST STATE

By agreeing to the establishment of a permanent diplomatic mission a state implicitly accepts certain obligations: it must provide such facilities and immunity as will enable the mission to function satisfactorily, and it must grant to those who work in the mission the personal privileges and immunity necessary for them to carry out their functions without fear or hindrance. These obligations are set out in Chapter 5 dealing with 'Diplomatic privileges and immunities'.

## THE CONDUCT OF DIPLOMATIC RELATIONS IN THE ABSENCE OF A FULL DIPLOMATIC MISSION OR WHEN DIPLOMATIC RELATIONS HAVE BEEN SEVERED

No state maintains a diplomatic mission in every capital in the world; most have to be selective, and balance their national interest against the cost involved. The problem of not having full diplomatic representation in a particular state can be resolved in any of four ways:

(a) by requesting a government which is represented by a permanent mission in the state concerned to act on its behalf, which it may do with the approval of that state. In these circumstances the head of the permanent mission would normally limit his activities to transmitting messages between the two governments concerned and dealing with consular matters; and if any conflict arose between the interests of his own government and those of the foreign government on whose behalf he was acting, the interests of his own government would prevail;

(b) by accrediting one of its heads of mission resident in another state as a non-resident or 'visiting' head of mission in the state concerned;

(c) by establishing a diplomatic mission headed by a duly accredited non-resident head of mission, but with a Chargé d'Affaires *ad interim* in charge. In practice, owing to the difficulty encountered by several states in finding adequate senior diplomatic staff for the posts they wish to fill, it is not uncommon for a host state to agree to such a mission being headed by a diplomat of lesser standing;

(d) by accrediting a very senior official (e.g. the Permanent Secretary of the Foreign Ministry) as a non-resident or 'visiting' head of mission in a number of states while maintaining his residence in his own capital.

In certain instances diplomatic missions may be withdrawn as a result of mutual agreement between the states concerned, for example on the grounds that changed circumstances have resulted in the missions being unnecessary or uneconomic. Missions may also be withdrawn as a deliberate act of foreign policy, and in the days of straightforward gunboat diplomacy the withdrawal of a mission with the consequent breaking off of diplomatic relations was a logical prelude to war; in practice, the threat of such action by a big power was usually sufficient to convince the smaller power that it was time that it reviewed its foreign policy. Today this manoeuvre is occasionally used, not so much as a threat but as a protest; but as such its effect is limited, and usually disproportionate to the inconvenience that it causes to all concerned.

Even when a mission is withdrawn and diplomatic relations formally broken off, contacts are rarely terminated: the states of the world are to an increasing extent interdependent, and diplomatic relations frequently carry on in varying degrees as before, but (provided the host state has no objection) through the intermediary

## Diplomatic relations

or 'good offices' of a state that is represented by a permanent mission in that country. In some cases only the head of the mission leaves: the remainder of the staff, by agreement with the host state, carry on their political, commercial and cultural activities in their customary premises but (in theory at least) as members of the staff of the 'protecting' mission which is looking after the interests of their country. They retain their personal diplomatic privileges and immunity, communicate with their government under privilege in the name of the 'protecting' mission, and continue to function normally except that they may not fly their national flag or display their national emblem on their official premises. If they display a flag or emblem it will be that of the 'protecting' mission.

# Chapter 2

# THE MINISTRY OF FOREIGN AFFAIRS

## ORGANISATION AND FUNCTIONS

The governments of all states include among their members one who is responsible for relations with other states and with international organisations. The extent of his personal responsibility varies from country to country, as does his title: Minister for Foreign Affairs, Secretary of State (USA), Secretary of State for Foreign and Commonwealth Affairs (UK), etc. The Minister's executive function is to implement the foreign policy of his government, and to manage its international relations. This he does with the help of the permanent staff of his Ministry and the heads of his own missions abroad, and through the intermediary of the heads of foreign missions accredited to his state.

The composition of Ministries varies considerably from country to country, but on the basis of the functions that they perform might be divided into the following sections, and grouped according to convenience:

*Political Affairs* – usually subdivided into regional departments, e.g. Latin America, Australasia.
*The United Nations* – including the provision of directives or 'briefs'.
*Other international and regional organisations* – including inter-departmental coordination and the provision of non-technical briefs.
*Treaties* – this section works in close relations with the legal department.
*Legal* – a separate department in the larger states; it normally deals with all international instruments and all questions of international law. Smaller countries may appoint part-time professional or academic advisers or obtain advice from a general Ministry of Justice. The legal department may advise both in matters of home and foreign affairs. In certain states a Department of International Law

exists as a separate entity from the Legal Department, the latter concerning itself with legal assistance, frontier problems, nationality law, national property abroad, etc.

*Protocol* – responsibility for all personal dealings with heads of foreign missions on such matters as privileges, immunities and formalities; also for the organisation of conferences, reception of visitors, etc.

*Trade and economic relations*
*Cultural relations*
*Disarmament*
*Press and Information* – this includes relations with foreign press representatives, and may also include the provision of information for the home news services and keeping the Ministry's missions abroad informed of events at home and abroad.
*Scientific*
*Personnel*
*Commodities*
*Consular relations*
*Administration, communications and security*
*Archives and library*

When a country maintains close international relations on a wide variety of matters of national concern its Ministry of Foreign Affairs would be overloaded and even technically out of its depth if it were to try to maintain a close control over the negotiations concerned. An example of this situation is the relationship between the countries of western Europe, where matters of defence, social welfare, health, economic relations, etc., are of close mutual concern, and policies are constantly under discussion and negotiation between the departmental experts rather than through the traditional channels of the Ministry of Foreign Affairs. But although a Ministry of Foreign Affairs may in many instances relinquish immediate responsibility to other departments, it has an essential coordinating function and must always remain responsible for background information, political advice, personal relationships and follow-up; and it must always be in a position to step in and take action, or at least make recommendations, if it considers that a particular department, in pursuing its particular interest, is in danger of losing sight of the national interest as a whole.

# RELATIONS WITH ITS OWN MISSIONS

The prime responsibility of a head of mission is to carry out the instructions of his Ministry and to report back to it the information that he is asked to provide. He is, however, expected to use his initiative in recommending the policy that he thinks his government should adopt, and also in reporting back information that he personally considers significant, whether he has been asked to do so or not. The relationship between Ministry and heads of mission is thus very much a matter of give and take, and the extent to which the Ministry or the mission dominates in the shaping of policy varies from country to country and in accordance with the national requirements and resources.

If policy decisions are reached essentially within the Ministry and the task of the head of mission is mainly that of implementing them, emphasis in terms of numbers of staff (and often ability) is likely to be placed on the Ministry, leaving fewer to serve abroad; but if policy-making is to be influenced strongly by the advice of the heads of mission, then the staff of the Ministry need be relatively few, and the overseas posts may be strongly manned. Staff distribution policy will also determine the length of time that diplomats serve abroad compared with the time that they spend at home, and there is a marked contrast not only between the policies of different countries but also between types of officers: for example, a commercial or press attaché for whom wide local contacts are essential might be of greatest value if his stay in a country were five years or longer, while for an embassy secretary the standard period might be three or four.

The arguments in favour of a diplomat remaining in a post for a lengthy period are:

(a) he – or of course she – (and his/her family) need time to settle down domestically before he can really concentrate on his work;
(b) he will have an adequate opportunity of getting to know and understand the country in which he is serving – its language, history, politics and national temperament;
(c) he will have time to make personal contacts and friendships;
(d) there will be a saving for the government of expense on travel and costs of transfer.

The main disadvantage is that he may become emotionally involved in the problems of the country in which he is living and serving, and so be unable to act and advise his own government in a detached and realistic manner. Also he is liable to find himself out of touch with sentiment and events in his home country.

The head of the personnel department has one of the most important tasks in the Ministry, deciding whom to send where and for how long. A diplomat is subject to a wide variety of pressures in different posts abroad, and some can cope with particular circumstances better than others: a posting that suits his temperament and personality is in many ways as important as one that suits his ability.

## RELATIONS WITH FOREIGN MISSIONS

The Ministry of Foreign Affairs (or its equivalent) is the channel through which all representations should be made to a government by another state, its diplomatic representative or an international organisation. If the enquiry is of an essentially technical or routine nature the Ministry may authorise the appropriate technical department to carry on further correspondence direct with the mission or organisation concerned; but the initial approach and all matters of substance are traditionally addressed to the Ministry.

In practice, with the great increase in the scope and extent of international cooperation since the establishment of the United Nations and regional economic and political groupings, there has been a tendency for home government departments to assume even greater responsibility for international negotiations within their particular field.

When a Minister for Foreign Affairs assumes office he writes to all the diplomatic representatives of foreign states and informs them accordingly, and subsequently arranges for each of them to call on him or (in a large capital) for a reception at which he can meet them. When he relinquishes the post he also advises them accordingly and gives them the name of his successor. In addition, the Minister informs the diplomatic representatives of his own country abroad of such moves.

The head of a diplomatic mission (unless he is a Chargé d'Affaires *en titre*) is the representative of one Head of State to another; and although it is no longer practical for him to claim the right of access to the Head of State, or, in many countries, to the head of government, he has by custom and courtesy the right of access to the Minister for Foreign Affairs at any time in order to discuss matters of concern between the two countries. Dealings of a routine matter, however, are normally carried out between the head of mission or a member of the diplomatic staff of the mission and the appropriate official in the Ministry of Foreign Affairs.

When a Minister for Foreign Affairs wishes to convey a message to another government he has two possible means of communication: through his country's own diplomatic representative in the foreign country concerned; or through that country's representative to the Minister's own government. (Since any government is the instrument of the Head of State, a head of mission may correctly be said to be the representative of one government to another.) Generally speaking a government makes formal approaches through its own representative abroad, but formal protests are often made to the foreign representative who is perhaps more immediately available; effectiveness being the obvious key to the choice of method. Sometimes both are used at the same time. By summoning a head of mission and speaking directly person-to-person, a Minister for Foreign Affairs can doubtless stress the extent of his displeasure when asking for a clarification, particularly if the time chosen for the summons is known to coincide with the diplomat's breakfast or golf.

# RELATIONS WITH THE DIPLOMATIC CORPS

Matters concerning the Diplomatic Corps in its entirety and the government of the state to which its members are accredited or assigned are dealt with by the senior head of mission (who is known as the Doyen) and the appropriate minister or chief of the Department of Protocol. The term 'Doyen' of the Corps Diplomatique might reasonably be transposed to 'Dean of the Diplomatic Body'; but common usage among English speakers is 'Dean of the Diplomatic Corps'.

In determining the appointment of the Dean or Doyen, the seniority of a head of mission is based on the length of time that he has continuously held his appointment at that post. In certain countries (usually predominantly Roman Catholic) the Apostolic Nuncio is always Dean; and the practice is not uncommon, especially in Latin America, for special provision to be made for Armed Services attachés by the appointment of protocol officers in the Ministry of Defence.

# Chapter 3

# THE DIPLOMATIC MISSION

## GENERAL OBSERVATIONS AND DEFINITIONS

A diplomatic mission consists of a diplomatic representative duly nominated by one state and accepted by another, together with his staff (if any), and established in the diplomatic capital of the state. As far as the receiving state is concerned there is only one person who may represent another state, and he is head (or acting head) of that mission who, as such, is entirely responsible for its activities; his staff, strictly speaking, have no direct representatives function and merely assist their head.

The terminology of diplomacy is often obscure and misleading, and the 1961 Vienna Convention on Diplomatic Relations usefully defined the staff of a diplomatic mission (with the French expression in brackets) as follows:

(a) The 'head of the mission' (*chef de mission*) is the person charged by the sending state with the duty of acting in that capacity;

(b) the 'members of the mission' (*membres de la mission*) are the head of the mission and the members of the staff of the mission;

(c) the 'members of the staff of the mission' (*membres du personnel de la mission*) are the members of the diplomatic staff, of the administrative and technical staff and of the service staff of the mission;

(d) the 'members of the diplomatic staff' (*membres du personnel diplomatique*) are the members of the staff of the mission having diplomatic rank;

(e) a 'diplomatic agent' (*agent diplomatique*) is the head of the mission or a member of the diplomatic staff of the mission;

(f) a 'member of the administrative and technical staff' (*membre du personnel administratif et technique*) is a member of the staff of the mission employed in the administrative or technical service of the mission;

(g) a 'member of the service staff' (*membre du personnel de service*) is a member of the staff of the mission in the domestic service of the mission;

(h) a 'private servant' (*domestique privé*) is a person who is in the domestic service of a member of the mission and who is not an employee of the sending state.

The term 'diplomatic agent', which formerly referred only to the head of a mission, now includes the members of the diplomatic staff of the mission; and 'the members of the diplomatic staff' are not only members of a diplomatic service, but also attachés, advisers and members of other ministries, provided that they hold diplomatic rank.

The term 'diplomatic rank' is not defined, but is used in this context to describe the range of appointments in a diplomatic mission which by tradition entitle the holders to full diplomatic privileges and immunities; and although the term 'diplomatic agent' is the correct word to describe the head of mission and members of the diplomatic staff of a mission, the commonly accepted (though less precise) terminology is 'diplomat'.

The functions of a mission are reflected in its structure, and the following pattern remains valid even if, as may happen in some instances, they are all performed by a single person:

The head of mission
Chancery
    Political work
    Administration and coordination
    Secretarial and archives
    Security
    Communications and other technical services
    Local staff
    Accounts
Commercial section
Consular section
Press and Information section
Military, Naval, Air and other specialist services.

# THE HEAD OF MISSION

The head of mission is responsible for all matters connected with his mission. He may, and does, delegate various functions to his staff, but he alone is responsible both to his own government and to the government to which he is accredited for the conduct of the mission.

Irrespective of the size of his staff there are certain basic priorities to which a head of mission normally devotes his personal attention:

(a) the formulation of diplomatic policy;
(b) transmitting to the host government the views of his own government on important matters of common interest and common policy, and acting as the channel of communication between the two in such matters;
(c) reporting to his Ministry on events of political or economic significance, whether they are of direct significance (e.g. the national budget or ministerial changes) or of indirect significance (e.g. changes and trends in social or economic conditions), and commenting on the views of third parties in the country (e.g. articles from the local press, opinions of other diplomats);
(d) being aware of the people of influence and the sources of national power in the state in which he is serving;
(e) conducting himself in his official and personal behaviour in such a way as to bring credit to his country;
(f) cultivating as wide and as varied a circle of friends as is possible in order to be able to fulfil (a), (c), (d) and (e) above).

The formulation of the diplomatic policy of a mission is a major responsibility of the head of mission, and in this he is assisted by his principal advisers – the heads of the various sections of his mission. The diplomatic policy of a mission can best be defined as the positive attitude adopted towards all matters relating to intercourse between the head of mission's own state and the one to which he is accredited. It is the product of political judgment, political sense and political wisdom, and is based on an intimate knowledge and understanding of the people and governments of the two states concerned. It may take the form of the head of mission recommending policies to his own government or seeking clarification of their instructions and suggesting a different line of approach; or alternatively suggesting to the government to which he is accredited that a communication that they have instructed him to refer to his government should be reconsidered. It is reflected in the advice given to visiting politicians or businessmen on how to approach people or problems, and is the function that differentiates a diplomatic mission from a post office.

# CHANCERY

## ADMINISTRATION AND COORDINATION

In the British diplomatic service a single officer (the Head of Chancery) is usually responsible for two important functions: the coordination of the activities of the mission and the oversight of the administration of the mission. In other services these tasks come under the Deputy Head of Mission or are divided between a senior secretary (political) and an administration officer. The Head of Chancery ensures that all correspondence is dealt with promptly and that all the various sections of the mission are properly coordinated; that the staff is properly organised and contented; and that communications and the premises of the mission are secure and adequately maintained. The welfare of his staff is a matter of particular concern, for the younger members and those who do not enjoy the privileges of being members of the diplomatic staff may find themselves subject to loneliness and its related ills.

One of the Head of Chancery's more important duties could be to compile and keep up to date files containing all the items of local information that an incoming head of mission or member of the staff might want to know.

Such files would normally include:

(a) The organisation of the Ministry of Foreign Affairs of the host state and any other departments or institutions with which the mission deals; which section deals with which matters; how to obtain an interview, whom to approach (and whom to avoid);

(b) a short account of recent local history;

(c) a 'Post Report' containing matters of domestic interest to members of the staff; medical, dental, travel and sporting facilities; climate; housing; domestic help; schools; churches, etc. (this would normally be sent to the Personnel Department at home for the briefing of future members of the mission);

(d) a list of personalities which would include distinguished or up-and-coming persons of influence in the political, military, administrative, industrial, commercial, academic and social sphere.

With such information at his disposal an incoming head of mission can quickly grasp the local situation and find his way around. In particular he can know straight away who is significant in relation to his country's interests; social blunders can be avoided, and entertaining (*q.v.*) greatly facilitated.

## SECRETARIAL AND ARCHIVES

Members of the secretarial and archives staff who deal with confidential matters are normally of the same nationality as the mission, though non-political sections (e.g. cultural or commercial) may employ local residents provided that they maintain a separate secretarial and archival section. The maintenance of an efficient and well-indexed system of records is a time-consuming occupation, but one of fundamental importance.

## SECURITY

The task of the security staff is to ensure that the premises of the mission are not entered unlawfully; that persons entering the building on business are not able to obtain confidential information; and that access to files and documents is restricted to those so entitled. The security staff are almost invariably of the same nationality as the mission.

## TECHNICAL AND COMMUNICATIONS

The technical staff are primarily concerned with communications. They are required to encode and decode, encypher and decypher, and operate and, when necessary, repair wireless transmitters and receivers (in those missions that have been granted permission by the host government to use this means of communication), fax and telex machines, encoding and decoding equipment, etc. Their work is of a confidential nature and they are invariably of the same nationality as the mission.

## LOCAL STAFF

Local staff are employed in non-confidential duties as part of the administrative and secretarial staff. They can be of immense value on account of their continuity of service and their knowledge of local customs, politics and personalities. They are commonly employed in the commercial, consular and information sections and as translators.

## ACCOUNTS

Accounts are unavoidable, and, if neglected, can cause more trouble than all the rest of the functions of the mission put together; a competent book-keeper (usually local staff) is employed where circumstances permit. A good accounting system has the advantage of enabling local bills to be settled promptly; failure to do so often resulting in ill-will that can undo much of the good relations established by the mission.

## COMMERCIAL SECTION

The task of the member in charge of the commercial section is to foster in every way possible the trading interests of his own country: to assist visiting businessmen, to reply to specific queries, and generally to provide all background information that will enable his country to formulate an appropriate trade policy and its businessmen to assess and take advantage of the local market. He studies in particular changes in the customs tariffs, quotas and import regulations, and the calling for tenders; and advises his head of mission if he should draw the host government's attention to any acts or changes in policy that might prove detrimental to his country's interests. While concentrating on his own country's interests he cannot avoid enquiries in the opposite sense from local businessmen, and these he will do his best to answer in the interests of good relations.

## CONSULAR SECTION

A consular office in a capital city normally comes directly under the control of the head of the diplomatic mission, and often occupies part of the premises of the mission; it is, however, in some respects a separate entity governed by its own regulations. Its functions and organisation are dealt with in a subsequent chapter.

## PRESS AND INFORMATION SECTION

The member of the staff in charge of the Press and Information section has to know what makes news in a particular country and who, locally, makes it, so that he may provide information concerning his country to the maximum effect. Apart from maintaining good relations with the producers of instant publicity – the press, radio and television – a press officer often finds it advantageous to circulate a news-sheet to persons who are known to be interested in and sympathetic to his country. He will usually need the services of a translator (local staff), for an article will only be acceptable if it is written in the language of the country in which it has to be used. It has always to be borne in mind that in many countries the Media has a significant influence on popular opinion, and this in turn influences a country's foreign policy decisions to an ever increasing extent.

# SERVICE AND SPECIALIST ATTACHÉS

Until quite recently there was a clear distinction between a career diplomat, who concerned himself with political relations, and an attaché, whose interests were limited to a particular field. The former was a member of the diplomatic service and in practice a link between his own Ministry of Foreign Affairs and that of the state to which he was accredited or assigned; the latter was a member of a different government department, and while coming under the auspices and control of the head of mission was primarily serving the interests of his own department. With the growing number of specialist personnel now needed in large diplomatic missions, however, the distinction between the two categories has lessened, and specialists in, for example, legal or labour matters may be either attachés or secretaries on the diplomatic staff. It is absolutely essential that their work should be closely coordinated with that of the mission as a whole.

## ARMED SERVICES ATTACHÉS

Armed Services attachés are normally regular members of the Armed Forces who are attached to a diplomatic mission for a limited period of time. One of the major functions of a Military, Naval or Air Force attaché is to report on developments in his particular field of interest to his particular branch of the services either directly or, in important matters, through his head of mission. He can, in certain instances, help with the purchase or sale of war materials, and in most countries will be invited to take part in military exercises.

## CULTURAL AND EDUCATIONAL ATTACHÉS

Cultural agreements were at one time the last resort of governments which could find nothing else to agree upon. Today the work of the cultural attaché can be of great value in fostering understanding and goodwill between states by arranging exchange visits of professional or occupational groups, or visits of world-class artists, by the award of scholarships, and in some instances by facilitating the study of his national language. It is sometimes the practice to appoint as attaché a person eminent in the field of a particular cultural activity; but in such instances it is also the practice to appoint a good administrator as his assistant. In some instances separate cultural and educational attachés are appointed.

## OTHER ATTACHÉS

The range of possible attachés is limited only by the interest of the states appointing them and the willingness of the states receiving them. Their titles are indicative of their function, and include: Labour, Agriculture, Fisheries, Scientific, Industrial, Civil Aviation, Public Relations, Recruitment, Tourism, Legal, Immigration, Shipping and Timber. Chaplains are an important member of certain missions, who may be members of the diplomatic staff and enjoy diplomatic status.

# ABSENCE OR INDISPOSITION OF A HEAD OF MISSION

If a head of mission is absent or otherwise unable to perform his functions (e.g. through serious illness), or if the post of head of mission is vacant, a member of the diplomatic staff of the mission (usually the next senior) will fill the post as Chargé d'Affaires *ad interim*. In these circumstances the head of mission or his Ministry informs the appropriate authorities of the host state of the change, and advises them when the head of mission resumes his functions. If no member of the diplomatic staff is available to take charge during the absence of a head of mission, a member of the administrative or technical staff may, with the approval of the host state, be appointed by his government to take charge of the current administrative business of the mission. If a Chargé d'Affaires *ad interim* is unable to continue his functions, he may not appoint a Chargé in his place: this can only be done by his Ministry of Foreign Affairs.

# APPOINTMENTS, ARRIVALS AND DEPARTURES

## NOTIFICATION OF APPOINTMENTS

Although it is only the appointment of heads of mission and frequently that of Military, Naval or Air Attachés that require the formal approval of the host state in advance, all other appointments of diplomatic staff must be notified to the Ministry of Foreign Affairs at the earliest opportunity.

## NOTIFICATION OF ARRIVALS AND DEPARTURES

The head of a mission should, where possible, advise the Protocol Department of the Ministry of Foreign Affairs well in advance of the date, place and time of the intended arrival or final departure of any member of the staff of the mission or of their families. In addition, in some countries it is the practice to provide the Consular Department of the Ministry with details of the engagement or discharge of any residents or nationals of the country in which the mission is situated.

## PROCEDURE ON ARRIVAL

On arrival at his post to take up his duties, a head of mission will be met by the Chief of Protocol (or his deputy). This will not, however, be the case in the event of his arrival coinciding with a national or religious holiday or (in an increasing number of countries) over a weekend or very early or very late in the day. He immediately informs the Minister for Foreign Affairs (as well, of course, as informing his own Minister) that he has arrived, and requests an appointment so that he may call on him and, according to the practice in a number of countries, present him with a copy of his credentials.

In the UK, for example, an Ambassador would do this by sending to the Secretary of State for Foreign and Commonwealth Affairs, by hand of the protocol representative who meets him, a letter on the following lines.

> Sir,
> I have the honour to inform you of my arrival in London on [date] in order to take up my duties as Ambassador of ............................... to the Court of St. James's.
> I should appreciate it if arrangements could be made for me to call on the appropriate Ministers and senior officials of the Foreign and Commonwealth Office and, in due course, for me to have an Audience with Her Majesty the Queen for the presentation of my credentials the Working Copies of which I enclose herewith [or] which have already been sent to your department.
> With the assurance of my highest consideration,
> I have the honour to be, Sir,

Your obedient Servant,
[Usual signature of Ambassador]

The Rt Hon. ....................,
Secretary of State for Foreign and Commonwealth Affairs,
Foreign and Commonwealth Office,
London SW1

According to UK practice the receipt of the working copy of the Ambassador's credentials (and of his predecessor's letter of recall where appropriate), together with the letter announcing his arrival, constitute the formal assumption of his duties.

If the head of mission holds the rank of Chargé d'Affaires *en titre* he will be accredited to the Minister for Foreign Affairs and will deliver to him his letter of appointment; but assuming, as is likely to be the case nowadays, that he holds the rank of Ambassador, his next call will be a ceremonial one on the Head of State (to present the original of his credentials), arrangements for which will usually be made through the head of the Department of Protocol. If it is the practice to deliver a formal speech at this audience, he should ensure that the Minister for Foreign Affairs has a copy of it in advance.

The procedure adopted by a state for the reception of a particular class of head of mission (i.e. Ambassador, Minister or Chargé d'Affaires) must be uniform in all cases.

Once a head of mission has officially assumed his functions he advises the Dean (Doyen) of the Diplomatic Corps and other heads of mission accordingly, and proceeds to call on them in accordance with the diplomatic protocol.

In a city of considerable diplomatic activity such as, for example, London, where the number of diplomatic missions has trebled in the past thirty years, the traditional practice for newly arrived heads of mission has been adapted to present-day circumstances. After paying courtesy calls on Ministers and senior officials of the Foreign and Commonwealth Office (usually within a week or ten days of arrival), heads of mission call on the Doyen of the Diplomatic Corps, a selected number of their fellow heads of mission (chosen, in order of seniority, according to the political interests and geographical position of the newcomer's country), and on prominent figures in British life of their own choosing. Because a new head of mission has entered *fully* on his functions by presenting to the FCO, on his arrival, the working copies of his credentials, his call on the Queen to present the credentials themselves is in the nature of a symbolic last act of the arrival procedure rather than (as in many other countries) an essential first act. Because of the Queen's absence from London, it can sometimes be a month or so before a new head of mission presents his credentials, but meanwhile he can, quite properly, circulate a note to other missions announcing his arrival and assumption of functions.

If a head of mission is replacing a colleague (as opposed to opening up a mission) he ensures that the appropriate procedure has been carried out with regard to his predecessor's *letter of recall*.


PROCEDURE ON DEPARTURE

Shortly before a head of mission relinquishes his post (except in the event of his recall having been requested by the host state) he sends a note announcing his recall to the Minister for Foreign Affairs and asks for an audience with the Head of State. This farewell audience is a private one and the departing head of mission may take the opportunity of presenting his letter of recall. It is the normal practice nowadays, however, to combine an outgoing head of mission's letter of recall (a formal document signed by the Head of State) with his successor's letter of credence.

A departing head of mission writes to the Dean of the Diplomatic Corps and to other heads of mission and informs them that he is leaving, e.g.

> Your Excellency (or Monsieur le Chargé d'Affaires),
> I have the honour to inform Your Excellency (you) that I shall be leaving ............................. [place] on ..................... [date], on the termination of my mission.
> Until the arrival of my successor, the direction of this Embassy will be assumed by Mr ..................... Counsellor [e.g.] of this Embassy, as Chargé d'Affairs ad interim.
> I should like to take this opportunity to express to Your Excellency (you) my sincere gratitude for your cooperation which has contributed to the good relations, both official and personal, which so happily exist between our two countries and our two missions.
> Please accept, Your Excellency (Monsieur le Chargé d'Affaires), the assurance of my highest (high) esteem.
>
> Ambassador's name
>
> His Excellency ....................., etc.
> (or Mr ....................., Chargé d'Affaires, etc.)

The head of mission's diplomatic functions come to an end either when he leaves the country or on an earlier date if this is specified in his note announcing his recall. (If he does not leave on the date specified it is customary for him, together with his family, to be allowed full privileges and immunities for a reasonable period until his departure.) He is normally seen off at his point of departure by a representative of the Department of Protocol (the Chief or his Deputy).

## THE DIPLOMAT

The diplomat needs to acquire all the normal attributes of his compatriots who are successful businessmen, administrators or civil servants, but he is a specialist in that he needs an added dimension: he must understand other countries, other cultures and other societies, and know what makes them tick. He must like people, and be genuinely interested in them.

He needs specialist knowledge, skills and qualities, which may be summarised as follows:

### SPECIALIST KNOWLEDGE

A knowledge and understanding of his own country: its geography, history and culture, its political, social, economic and demographic structure and institutions, its human and economic resources – agriculture, industry, finance – in short the determinants of its foreign policy priorities.

A similar knowledge and understanding of other states and regions, priority being given to his neighbours, his region and super-states.

A knowledge of the mechanism and procedures of international intercourse. This involves a knowledge of the worldwide network of diplomatic missions and consular posts, their functions, their practice and structure; the worldwide network of private and state trading and financial establishments and how they operate; and the existing inter-governmental institutions, global and regional, for international political, social and economic cooperation; also the code of public international law which establishes rules of behaviour between states and the laws regulating international institutions. Not least, he should have an understanding of the social and political consequences of the current 'Media Revolution'.

### FUNCTIONAL SKILLS

Skill in negotiating and in day-to-day diplomacy
Skill in observing, analysing and reporting

## The diplomatic mission

Skill in representation
Skill in the management of a mission
Skill in communication and public diplomacy
Cross-cultural skills


## SPECIALIST QUALITIES

Political awareness
Personal acceptability
Intellectual curiosity and the drive to go on learning
Intellectual versatility
Leadership
Common sense

The compendium of knowledge and the table of virtues required for the perfect diplomat are rarely found in one man: which is perhaps just as well for those ordinary mortals who would have the trying task of working or living with him.

# Chapter 4
# PROTOCOL AND PROCEDURE

## ORDERS OF PRECEDENCE

A diplomat is concerned with four orders of precedence:

## 1.  PRECEDENCE BETWEEN HEADS OF DIPLOMATIC MISSIONS

The precedence of a head of mission is based on the class into which he falls:

Ambassador, High Commissioner or Apostolic Nuncio or Pro-Nuncio; Envoy Extraordinary and Minister Plenipotentiary or Inter-nuncio (a rank rarely used);
Chargé d'Affaires *en titre* (titular or *en pied*).

Within each class, seniority is based on the date on which the head of mission assumed his duties as such. This is either the date on which he presented his credentials to the Head of State, or alternatively the date on which he notified his arrival to the Ministry of Foreign Affairs and sent or handed to the Minister or Ministry a copy of his credentials, depending on the practice of the country. In most countries the date is that of the presentation to the Head of State, but in some, including the UK (see p. 24), it is the date of handing over the copy of credentials.

If two heads of mission present their credentials on the same day precedence may be determined either by the place in the alphabet of the first letter of the state (in French) of the representative concerned; or, more commonly, by the relative times of day they officially commenced their functions. Whichever practice of determining precedence is adopted by a state, it must be applied consistently, and not altered without prior notification.

In certain states the diplomatic representative of the Holy See takes precedence over all other heads of mission of the same category.

At gatherings at which all heads of mission are present a Chargé d'Affaires *en titre* will follow heads of mission of ambassadorial rank, and Chargés d'Affaires *ad interim* will come third, each Chargé taking precedence within his class according to the date of his assumption of duty. When other members of the diplomatic staff of a mission (including spouses) are present they take their place with the head of mission or Chargé in accordance with his precedence.

Precedence is not affected by a head of mission's credentials becoming temporarily invalid owing to the death of the Head of State who signed or accepted them.

## 2. INDIVIDUAL PRECEDENCE WITHIN A MISSION

The individual precedence of members of the 'political' staff below head of mission is:

Minister Plenipotentiary
Minister-Counsellor
Counsellor
First Secretary
Second Secretary
Third Secretary

The place of service and specialist attachés is determined by individual missions. They usually come before a First Secretary but rarely above the diplomat next senior to the head of mission. The precise order of precedence is normally found in the diplomatic list which every state receiving diplomatic representatives produces, though in certain states the list is arranged in functional sections. It is the responsibility of the head of mission to notify the Ministry of Foreign Affairs of the precedence of the members of his mission.

## 3. INDIVIDUAL PRECEDENCE *INTER SE* OF DIPLOMATS AT FORMAL OR DIPLOMATIC FUNCTIONS

Individual precedence at formal or diplomatic functions is based on rank, and is as follows:

Apostolic Nuncio (in those countries where he is Doyen *ex officio*)
Ambassador, High Commissioner, Apostolic Nuncio or Pro-Nuncio
Envoy Extraordinary and Minister Plenipotentiary
Chargé d'Affaires (*en titre*)
Chargé d'Affaires (*ad interim*)
Minister Plenipotentiary
Minister-Counsellor
Counsellor
First Secretary
Second Secretary
Third Secretary

Service and specialist attachés are usually placed immediately after Counsellors, but practice varies.

## 4. PRECEDENCE OF HEADS OF MISSION WITHIN THE NATIONAL ORDER OF PRECEDENCE

Heads of mission are placed according to custom, but usually after members of the cabinet and the presidents of the legislative assemblies. In the United Kingdom heads of mission of ambassadorial rank are placed eighth after the Sovereign and close members of the Royal Family in the national order of precedence (after the Lord Privy Seal); and Chargés d'Affaires *en titre* according to courtesy.

## THE DIPLOMATIC LIST

The Diplomatic List is a record of the names and designation of (a) the heads of diplomatic missions accredited to a state at a particular date, together with the names and diplomatic rank of the members of the diplomatic staff of their mission, and (b) other institutions and individuals received in a diplomatic capacity (e.g. United Nations senior staff).

Also shown is the address of the mission and sometimes the residences of the diplomats; whether or not they are married; whether or not their spouses have accompanied them; and in some countries the names of unmarried daughters over the age of eighteen.

If the post of head of mission is temporarily vacant the designation of the holder is shown with the word 'vacant'. If the head of mission is non-resident, his place of residence is indicated after his name and the address of his mission and (usually) residence are given.

It is customary to add a list of heads of mission in order of their precedence (naming the Doyen), together with a list of the national days of the states represented in the host state.

The Diplomatic List is regularly revised and reprinted (the interval depending on the size of the state and the rate of diplomatic turnover); states are listed alphabetically (usually in the language of the issuing state); and the responsibility for the correctness of the information it contains rests jointly with the host government (in practice with the Department of Protocol) and the heads of diplomatic missions: both have a vested interest in the accuracy of the List, if only because it is used for reference by both parties, and because it is *prima facie* evidence of the right to diplomatic status.

The List does not normally have any security rating, and in some countries it is on sale to the public. It is issued free to all foreign missions and diplomatic agents, and to ministers and officials of the host government who may need to refer to it, e.g. customs and immigration officials, police and mayors, as well as to the heads of the issuing government's missions abroad.

In certain instances a combined Diplomatic and Consular List is issued containing, in addition, details of career and honorary consular officers; otherwise a separate Consular List is sometimes issued, depending on need.

# CORRESPONDENCE AND COMMUNICATION BETWEEN DIPLOMATIC MISSIONS AND THE HOST GOVERNMENT

All formal communications between a diplomatic mission and the foreign government in whose capital it is situated are made (a) by or on behalf of the head of mission, and (b) to the Ministry of Foreign Affairs (or its equivalent), except where special permission has been given for dealing with another department, or in the case of specialist attachés who are by custom permitted to deal direct with the relevant department on technical (but not policy) matters. In practice, the complexity of modern diplomacy has reduced the strict formalities in many countries.

## PERSONAL INTERVIEWS

The Minister for Foreign Affairs is customarily accessible to heads of mission, and appointments are usually made by telephone. Such top-level approaches are normally limited to matters of special importance; those of lesser importance are best dealt with by the head of mission or a member of the diplomatic staff of the mission arranging (once again by telephone) to see an appropriate member of the ministry staff. Ministers and ministry officials are normally very busy people, and tend to be sympathetic to visiting diplomats who, after the initial courtesies, are brief and to the point, and take their leave when there is no further business to conduct.

## WRITTEN CORRESPONDENCE

*(a) The Official Note in the third person*
The customary method of correspondence between a diplomatic mission and a Ministry of Foreign Affairs is the Official Note. The note is typed in a recognised international language on official paper headed with the national crest and address, and begins as follows:

> The ............................ Embassy presents its compliments to the Ministry of Foreign Affairs and has the honour to inform them that . . . [or] to bring to their attention the following matter . . .

The substance of the note then follows, and the document terminates with a formula on the following lines:

> The Embassy takes [or avails itself of] this opportunity of assuring the Ministry of its highest consideration.

> Date               [Sender's initials and Embassy stamp]

In some countries (e.g. the United States of America) this final courtesy is omitted.

The Official Note is also the standard form of communication between Diplomatic Missions.

*(b) The note verbale*
The *note verbale* is normally used to clarify or confirm points raised in a previous conversation or to list items which one could not expect to be recalled precisely. It is written in the third person and its general form is that of the official note.

*(c) The Official Letter in the first person*
A less formal approach to a Minister for Foreign Affairs (by a head of mission) or to an official in the Ministry (by a member of the diplomatic staff of a mission) is the letter in the first person. This is written on correspondence paper with the address and date at the top, and would be on the following lines:

## Protocol and procedure

### Head of mission to Minister for Foreign Affairs

An official letter from a head of mission to a Minister of Foreign Affairs usually begins:

'Your Excellency' or sometimes just 'Sir' or 'Excellency', followed by:

I have the honour . . .

*and ends with the sentence*:

I avail myself of the opportunity to assure Your Excellency of my highest consideration

*or*

Accept, Excellency, the renewed assurances of my highest consideration.

[Name of sender]

Alternatively, and depending on the Ambassador's relationship with the Minister, a letter might begin 'My dear Minister', and end with the words 'Yours sincerely'. This less formal approach is used in the UK since no British Minister or official there is properly addressed as 'Excellency'.

If the letter is addressed in the form 'Your Excellency', it ought strictly to continue in the same way, e.g. 'My government has studied Your Excellency's proposal . . .' However, such phraseology can become tedious, and the judicious and occasional use of the second person (you, your) is permissible, and avoids pomposity.

### Official to official

As a general rule correspondence between officials begins, 'My dear (name of addressee)', and ends 'Yours sincerely (name of sender)'.

### (d) Methods of providing records of verbal discussions

Heads of mission are frequently instructed by their governments to 'make representations' to the Ministry of the country to which they are accredited or to ask for clarification of an issue. This necessitates a personal visit during which the diplomat 'states his case', and in order that there can be no room for doubt as to the purpose of his visit, he leaves behind a summary of his remarks. This may take the form of:

An *aide-mémoire* which explains a government's action or point of view, or puts forward a proposition. It is headed 'Aide-

Mémoire' and bears the date at the end, but has no signature, address or Embassy stamp.

or

A *bout de papier* which is typed on paper without heading, signature or date, the theory being that its provenance could be denied if necessary. It is thus less 'official' than the *aide-mémoire*.

Diplomats may wish to put forward a tentative suggestion at a conference, or may be instructed by their government to make representations on a matter of great delicacy, about which their own Ministry does not yet wish to take a stand. The diplomat may then choose to discuss the issue and leave a *non-paper* in which the matter is clarified in a non-committal way.

*(e) Rejection of a note or letter*

If a Ministry of Foreign Affairs considers that a communication from another government is offensive in any way it may 'refuse to accept' it, even though it has already taken delivery of it and studied it. In these circumstances the Ministry – or invariably the Minister in such a serious situation – would summon the appropriate head of mission and hand back to him the document concerned informing him at the same time that it was unacceptable to his government.

# DEMONSTRATIONS

A diplomatic mission may find itself approached by a group of people asking for an interview with the Ambassador, or a member of his staff. An embassy thus approached has various options, the last being most commonly adopted:

- to keep the door shut,
- to accept the petition without comment,
- to invite the spokesman/men of the group in and explain the home government's position.

If the demonstration appears to be getting out of hand the Chief of Protocol (or, better still, the Police Diplomatic Protection Unit, if such exists) should be advised without delay: 'The receiving State is under a special duty to . . . prevent any disturbance of the peace of the mission or impairment of its dignity' (1961 Vienna Convention on Diplomatic Relations, Article 22, paragraph 2).

# FLAGS

Heads of mission are entitled to fly their national flag on their residence and the premises of their mission at all times, and it is the practice to do so to mark (a) their own national occasions, and (b) those of the state in which they are situated. They are also entitled to fly their national flag on their official car, although many choose to do so only on formal occasions or in dangerous situations.

On occasions when national mourning is officially prescribed, whether in the sending state or in the host state, flags are flown at half mast. They are normally flown in this manner only on the day of the funeral; but in the event of the death of a Sovereign it is customary for them to be flown from the day of death until (and including) the day of the funeral except on the date of the proclamation of the accession of the new Sovereign.

Traditionally flags are raised first thing in the morning (8 a.m.) and lowered at sunset.

Consular officers who include a port within their consular area are normally permitted – subject to any existing convention, and dependent on local custom – to fly their national flag on a boat (at the bow) when on official duty. It is also common practice for heads of consular posts to fly their national flag on their official car when making official visits to the local authorities or when they are invited to take part in ceremonies or festivities in their official capacity; but the precise conditions are often regulated by a consular convention. The flying of the national flag on a consular post may be prohibited if the premises are situated in the same city as the diplomatic mission.

On the occasion of the visit of a distinguished foreign guest, the national flag of the visitor's state and that of the host state are often flown at the same place, e.g. on either side of a saluting base or platform. In this instance the flag pole on the right hand of a person sitting on the platform would be the 'guest' one: and as such would fly the visitor's flag.

When a number of flags of different countries are flown from individual flagstaffs the place of honour should be assigned to the national flag, the others being arranged alternately to right and left of this central point (looking outwards from the site) in the alphabetical order of the countries represented.

# DRESS

The rules regarding dress for diplomats vary considerably between countries, and depend largely on tradition, custom and climate; the increasing trend being towards informality. There are, however, certain standard forms of dress which it is useful to be aware of (in addition to the diplomatic uniform or national dress that diplomats of certain states wear); these are normally indicated when invitation cards are sent, and for male diplomats are:

## MORNING COAT

Occasionally worn for daytime ceremonies, especially in the open, e.g. farewells to, or arrivals of, distinguished visitors.

Black tail coat; black waistcoat and black high silk hat for solemn occasions, alternatively grey waistcoat and grey top hat for festivities; white shirt, black striped 'pepper and salt' trousers; stiff turndown (i.e. plain) collar; grey tie, black shoes. Medal ribbons are not worn, but full-size medals are worn on the left breast if the occasion demands, e.g. military or remembrance.

## TAIL COAT ('WHITE TIE' OR FULL EVENING DRESS)

Usually restricted to formal evening functions such as dinners, balls or receptions; occasionally for more formal indoor ceremonies during the day (e.g. the presentation of credentials in the UK because it is the highest form of civilian national dress).

Long black tail coat; white waistcoat; stiff (starched) white shirt; wing collar; white bow tie; black trousers with two black silk stripes. Black silk hat; black patent leather shoes; miniatures of decorations and orders (the ribbon of any neck decoration going under the white tie, and the sash of an order going across the white waistcoat).

## DINNER JACKET ('BLACK TIE' OR 'SMOKING')

For informal evening functions.

Black jacket with silk-faced lapels; black trousers with one silk stripe; white shirt (usually soft with soft collar); black bow tie; black patent leather shoes. Miniatures of decorations and medals are worn where indicated on the invitation card.

The greater the degree of informality of the evening (and the climate), the greater is the liberty with regard to dress. In some situations cummerbunds (black, or sometimes maroon, silk sashes) are worn with dinner jackets; also coloured bow ties. White tuxedos are, in some countries, worn when the climate so demands.

## NATIONAL DRESS

Appropriate national dress is suitable for all diplomatic functions.

# STATE CEREMONIES

It usually falls to the Chief of the Department of Protocol to plan and execute arrangements for state ceremonies and these (assuming the once-and-for-all nature of independence celebrations) are most commonly: inaugurations, visits, anniversaries of national significance and funerals.

On all the above occasions (funerals being a possible exception) detailed plans are produced several weeks, even months, in advance and the Ministry would make a point of consulting with the Dean of the Diplomatic Corps if the Corps as a whole would be involved.

The cooperation of various organisations is essential for most functions, and it is usual to create an *ad hoc* planning and co-ordinating committee which might include representatives of the police (for parking and the regulation of traffic); the army (for a band and guard of honour); the press relations office and civic authorities; and, if foreign visitors are expected in any number, representatives of the customs, immigration and airports.

On the occasion of the visit of a foreign Head of State or member of the government or other person of distinction, the head of mission of the state concerned is invited to all the official functions and entertainments which the visitor attends; and in return the visitor offers hospitality at his head of mission's residence or an appropriate place for the corresponding dignitary in the host country (e.g. Head of State to Head of State, Foreign Minister to Foreign Minister, Head of Church to Head of Church).

A formal diplomatic visit begins when the visitor arrives in the diplomatic capital of the state (which normally must be his first objective) and it is there that the official reception takes place. The visitor's national anthem will be played, the guard of honour inspected, and compliments paid to the host's flag. If, however, the port, airport, or frontier post by which the visitor enters the state is some distance from the capital, the visitor is met by members of the local authority and an official representative who accompanies him to the capital. A procession with motor-cycle or horse escort is then arranged with the visitors riding in a carriage or motor car (depending on the distance involved). The general rule for the seating of state visitors in carriages and cars in a procession is that they are placed in the vehicles in descending order of precedence with the senior person in each vehicle seated behind the flag.

It is a recognised practice that the host of a state visit should be invited to return to visit to the other's capital within a reasonable time.

## OFFICIAL MOURNING

The observance of official mourning may be declared (a) by a head of mission's own government, in which event it applies to him and to the members of the staff of the mission; or (b) by the host government, in which case it applies to the Diplomatic Corps as a whole.

In the former instance, which might be occasioned by the death of the Head of State, the head of government or a member of the royal family or by a national catastrophe, a head of mission would receive instructions from his Ministry concerning the period of official mourning, the flying of the flag at half mast, etc. During this time he and members of the staff of his mission would wear black ties or their equivalent (ladies being appropriately dressed); and he would as far as possible refrain from giving or attending social engagements. Previously arranged official commitments might justifiably be cancelled, but state functions would have to be attended. Private functions, if given, would be unostentatious and relatively solemn. A 'condolences' book would be available at the Embassy or sometimes at the head of mission's residence to receive the signatures of persons wishing to express their sympathy, together with a tray for cards. In certain instances a photograph of the deceased is displayed surrounded by black ribbon; and black-edge stationery used for correspondence for a limited period of time.

In the event of official mourning being declared in the host country, the Diplomatic Corps acts as a body and receives its guidance through the Doyen who would be in close touch with the Chief of the Department of Protocol. Its members would be required to fly their flags at half mast for a given period, and to cancel all but the most informal gatherings. They would be expected to attend official ceremonies and generally to behave in conformity with the solemnity of the times. Heads of Mission would individually send formal letters of sympathy to the Minister for Foreign Affairs, and all members of the diplomatic staff of a mission would leave their cards marked 'p.c.' (*pour condoléances*) at the Ministry where a suitable receptacle would be provided, together with a condolences book.

If a distinguished national of a diplomatic colleague's state dies, heads of mission would express their condolences in a similar fashion, but there would be no general mourning. They would similarly express their condolences – by letter or by card, and by attendance at the funeral – on the death of a diplomatic colleague.

A note to the other diplomatic missions might take the following form:

> The Embassy of .............................. presents its compliments to the Diplomatic Missions accredited to the Court of St James's and in deep sorrow has the duty to inform them that ..................... died on ......
>
> A Book of Condolence will be opened at the Embassy .............................. (address) .............................. from Thursday 9 to Friday 10 September ......, between the hours of 10.00 a.m. and 2.00 p.m.
>
> The Embassy of .............................. avails itself of this opportunity to renew to the Diplomatic Missions accredited to the Court of St James's the assurance of its highest consideration.

# Chapter 5
# DIPLOMATIC PRIVILEGES AND IMMUNITIES

The privileged position of diplomats in society is traditional, but it is not for this reason that it continues to be respected; it is because representatives of a state can only carry out their diplomatic functions satisfactorily if they are utterly free from pressures, whether legal, physical or moral, that the state in which they are serving may be able to impose on them. In the majority of peaceful law-abiding countries the privileges and immunities to which they are entitled may appear pointless and excessive, and thus may cause resentment on the part of the host population; but in exceptional times and in exceptional countries it is only the recognition of mutually applicable privileges and immunities that enables diplomatic relations to be maintained.

Privileges and immunities are applicable both to the diplomatic mission and its functions, and to the individual.

The privileges and immunities accorded to diplomatic missions and their functions are also applicable to the United Nations and its functions under the 1946 Convention on the Privileges and Immunities of the United Nations, though the application of the Convention varies in different states.

The following is a summary of the principles contained in the 1961 Vienna Convention on Diplomatic Relations which has been accepted by an overwhelming majority of the members of the United Nations as representing an internationally agreed codification of modern diplomatic law.

## PRIVILEGES AND IMMUNITIES IN RESPECT OF THE MISSION AND ITS FUNCTIONS
### INVIOLABILITY AND IMMUNITY OF PREMISES AND PROPERTY

The premises of a mission and the private residence of the head of a mission are inviolable, as are those of members of the diplomatic

be provided by his Ministry or head of mission with a document indicating his status and the number of packages constituting the diplomatic bag. Where there is no regular diplomatic courier a state or mission may designate an individual – often an official of appropriate nationality who is making the journey for other reasons – as a diplomatic courier for a specific journey. Provided that he is furnished with the appropriate documents by his Ministry or head of mission he will be granted the same immunities and personal inviolability as a regular courier until such time as he has delivered the diplomatic bag in his charge. In normal circumstances a diplomatic bag may be entrusted to the captain of an aircraft, provided he enters or leaves the country through an authorised place of entry. A member of the mission concerned is entitled to hand the bag directly and freely to the captain, and similarly to receive it from him. The captain concerned must be provided with a document stating the number of packages constituting the bag; but he himself is not considered as being a diplomatic courier.

When communications between a state and its diplomatic mission have to pass through a third state, that state must furnish the same inviolability as is accorded by the receiving state. Diplomatic bags properly identified are inviolable while in transit through third states, as are diplomatic couriers. Couriers must however obtain any appropriate visas.


## EXEMPTION FROM TAXATION

A diplomatic mission is exempt from all national, regional and municipal dues and taxes in respect of the mission premises, whether owned or leased, except for those charges which represent payment for specific services rendered (e.g. water, electricity, refuse collection). This exemption does not extend to persons entering into contracts with a head of mission or his government – for which reason such contracts usually stipulate that it is the head of the mission or his government who are responsible for any rates or taxes on the premises.

A diplomatic mission is also exempt from dues and taxes in respect of any fees and charges that it levies as part of the normal functions of a mission.


## RIGHT TO IMPORT, AND EXEMPTION FROM CUSTOMS DUTIES

A diplomatic mission is entitled to import (subject to existing laws) articles for the official use of the mission, and is exempt from customs and other similar duties in respect of such articles. It is not exempt from charges for related services, e.g. storage or cartage. Goods imported duty free may not be sold or otherwise disposed of in the host state except in accordance with the conditions laid down by the state.

# PERSONAL PRIVILEGES AND IMMUNITIES

## GENERAL PROVISIONS

*Full diplomatic privileges and immunities* are applicable to (a) diplomats, and (b) members of their families forming part of their household provided they are not nationals or permanent residents of the state in which the diplomat is serving.

The interpretation of the term 'family' varies between states. The spouse and minor children of the diplomat are always included. Normally a diplomat who is a bachelor or widower or not accompanied by his wife would be entitled to count his mother or sister as part of the family if they are living with him; sons and daughters for whom the diplomat is legally responsible are included, as are widowed mothers.

*Limited diplomatic privileges and immunities* are afforded to three categories of members of the staff of a mission: those who are nationals or permanent residents of the state in which they are serving; members of the administrative and technical staff; and private servants of members of the mission.

As a counterpart to the enjoyment of immunity a diplomat may not practice for profit any professional or commercial activity in the state in which he is serving.

It is customary (but not universally accepted) practice for members of diplomatic missions to be issued with diplomatic identity cards by the host state. These carry the photograph and signature of the holder, together with whatever instructions the host state may see fit to add for the benefit of its officials with regard to the privileges, facilities and immunities which should be accorded to the bearer.

The immunity granted to a diplomat and members of his family by the host state does not exempt them from the jurisdiction of their own state.

## DURATION OF PRIVILEGES AND IMMUNITIES

Personal privileges and immunities apply from the moment the member of a mission enters the host country to take up his post or, if already in the country, from the moment his appointment is notified to the appropriate Ministry. Privileges and immunities come to an end when he leaves the country on the conclusion of his functions, or (if he does not leave immediately) after a reasonable interval of time (e.g. 4–6 weeks in the UK); but immunity from jurisdiction in respect of acts carried out in the course of his official duty has no limit in time. Immunity from jurisdiction in respect of any act carried out in a private capacity, however, does not continue after the conclusion of the diplomat's functions. In the event of the death of a member of a mission, the members of his family continue to enjoy the privileges and immunities to which they were entitled for a reasonable period of time sufficient to enable them to leave the country.

# FULL PRIVILEGES AND IMMUNITIES

## PERSONAL INVIOLABILITY AND PROTECTION

All diplomats enjoy personal inviolability, and members of their family forming part of their household similarly enjoy inviolability provided that they are not nationals or permanent residents of the host state. A state which accepts the establishment of a foreign diplomatic mission is bound to ensure complete protection to all members of that mission and to their families against physical violence whatever its source, and from attacks on their dignity and freedom.

## IMMUNITY FROM CRIMINAL JURISDICTION

A diplomat and members of his family forming part of his household (provided that they are not nationals or permanent residents of the host state) are immune from the criminal jurisdiction of the host state.

## IMMUNITY FROM CIVIL AND ADMINISTRATIVE JURISDICTION

A diplomat and members of his family forming part of his household (provided they are not nationals or permanent residents of the host state) are immune from civil and administrative jurisdiction in the host state except in the case of:

(a) a real action (i.e. an action to claim ownership or possession) relating to private immovable property situated in the host state, unless he holds it on behalf of the state he serves for the purposes of the mission;

(b) an action relating to succession in which he is involved as executor, administrator, heir or legatee as a private person and not on behalf of the state he serves;

(c) an action relating to any professional or commercial activity exercised by him in the host state outside his official function. This limitation applies in practice to his spouse and family.

## WAIVER OF DIPLOMATIC IMMUNITY

The immunity from jurisdiction of an individual entitled to such protection may be waived only by his government. A waiver of immunity from civil or administrative proceedings does no more than allow the person concerned to stand trial; a second and specific waiver is required before the judgement can be put into effect.

## COUNTERCLAIMS

If legal proceedings are started by a person enjoying diplomatic immunity he is not entitled to claim immunity from jurisdiction in respect of any counterclaim directly connected with the principal claim.

## INVIOLABILITY OF CORRESPONDENCE

The papers and correspondence of a diplomat and of members of his family forming part of his household (provided that they are not nationals or permanent residents of the host state) are inviolable.

## INVIOLABILITY OF PROPERTY

The property of a diplomat and of members of his family forming part of his household (provided that they are not nationals or permanent residents of the host state) is inviolable.

## EXEMPTION FROM LIABILITY FOR PUBLIC SERVICE

A diplomat and members of his family forming part of his household (provided that they are not nationals or permanent residents of the host state) are exempt from all personal and public services and from military obligations such as requisitioning, billeting or military contributions and from jury service.

## EXEMPTION FROM LIABILITY TO SERVE AS A WITNESS

A diplomat and members of his family forming part of his household (provided that they are not nationals or permanent residents of the host state) are not obliged to give evidence as witnesses (but in many cases do so in order to assist justice).

## EXEMPTION FROM NATIONAL AND LOCAL TAXATION

A diplomat and members of his family forming part of his household (provided that they are not nationals or permanent residents of the host state) are exempt from all dues and taxes, personal or real, national, regional or municipal, except for:

(a) Indirect taxes of a kind normally incorporated in the price of goods or services, e.g. value-added tax (though in some instances a refund of such taxes and excise duties is made on a reciprocal basis or to promote sales of goods manufactured in the receiving state).

(b) Dues and taxes on private immovable property situated in the territory of the host state, unless it is held on behalf of the sending state for the purposes of the mission.

(c) Estate, succession or inheritance duties levied by the host state, subject to the provisions referred to in Article 39 of the Vienna Convention. Generally speaking, such duties are not levied on an individual's movable property provided that its presence in the receiving state could reasonably be related to his official functions, and provided that he or she was not a permanent resident or national of the state concerned.

(d) Dues and taxes on private income originating in the host state, and capital taxes levied on commercial undertakings in that state.

(e) Charges levied for specific services rendered. (In UK practice this covers one-quarter approximately of local authority rates or taxes relating to services such as roads, street lighting and refuse collection from which a diplomat is deemed to derive direct benefit).

(f) Registration, court or record fees, mortgage dues and stamp duty in respect of immovable property (except for immovable property required as part of the premises of the mission in which case fees and dues are payable only in respect of specific services rendered).

## EXEMPTION FROM CUSTOMS DUTIES

A diplomat and members of his family forming part of his household (provided that they are not nationals or permanent residents of the host state) are entitled (in accordance with local regulations, which must not defeat diplomatic privilege) to import articles for their personal use, including articles required for the upkeep of their establishment, and are exempt from customs and other similar duties in respect of such articles. They are, however, liable to related charges for services, e.g. storage and cartage; and must comply with the regulations of the host state in respect of any articles imported duty-free that they subsequently sell or otherwise dispose of.

## EXEMPTION FROM SOCIAL SECURITY PROVISIONS

A diplomat and members of his family forming part of his household (provided that they are not nationals or permanent residents of the host state) are exempt from the social security provisions of the host state. Private servants in the sole employ of a diplomat are also exempt, provided that they are not nationals or permanent residents of the host state and that they are covered by the social security provisions of their own state; and a diplomat is obliged to comply with the social security provisions in force in respect of any person he employs who is not so exempt. In some states he may be permitted to participate in their social security scheme if he so wishes; and in others his position may be covered by an existing agreement between the host state and his own state.

## EXEMPTION FROM INSPECTION OF PERSONAL LUGGAGE

A diplomat and members of his family forming part of his household (provided that they are not nationals or permanent residents of the host state) are exempt from the inspection of personal luggage, unless there are serious grounds for believing that it contains articles that do not come within the scope of the privileges permitted, or illegal imports or exports. In this event the inspection is conducted only in the presence of the diplomat or of his authorised representative.

## FREEDOM OF TRAVEL

All members of the staff of a diplomatic mission are entitled to travel freely and without restriction in the state in which they are serving, except in those areas to which access is limited on grounds of national security. This principle is not always adhered to, and certain states limit the freedom of certain diplomats to special travel zones; and in such cases a policy of reciprocity is usually adopted.

## TRAVEL THROUGH A THIRD STATE

Provided that they have any necessary visas, diplomats and members of their family, whether travelling with them or separately, are entitled to inviolability and all other immunities necessary to ensure a safe journey when passing through a third state on their way to or from a post. To ensure this they should be provided by their Ministry with a letter (preferably in the language of the third state or states) giving the purpose of their journey; or with a diplomatic visa issued by a diplomatic or consular representative of that state. It is not normal for their luggage to be inspected, and the authorities should have very good reasons before doing so.

## RECIPROCAL OBLIGATIONS OF DIPLOMATS

The granting of privileges and immunities by a state implies the acceptance of a high standard of responsibility and integrity on the part of the recipient. He may not interfere in the internal affairs of that state nor allow official premises to be put to any purpose other than their proper and recognised function; and he should not take advantage of his immunity from the jurisdiction of the courts to disregard its laws in such matters as motor-car accidents, speeding and parking.

## DIPLOMATIC PASSPORTS

Diplomatic passports are issued by most states (but not the UK) to those of their nationals who are entitled to diplomatic immunity. They are usually taken not as evidence of entitlement to immunity (this being a function *prima facie* of the Diplomatic List), but as evidence of appointment only; they nevertheless often serve a useful purpose. Identity cards may be issued by the receiving state for the same purpose.

## REPRESENTATIVES TO INTERNATIONAL ORGANISATIONS

In certain cases resident (and sometimes non-resident) representatives of states to international organisations are entitled to the same privileges and immunities as diplomats. Representatives to the United Nations and its Specialised Agencies normally receive a wide range of privileges and immunities under the 1946 Convention on the Privileges and Immunities of the United Nations and the similar Convention regarding the Specialised Agencies. The few most senior officers on the staffs of these organisations are entitled to the full range of diplomatic privileges and immunities (unless they are nationals or permanent residents of the receiving state); the other staff members of the organisations enjoy more limited privileges and immunities. In the case of other organisations, such matters are normally included in the Agreement establishing the organisation or in an Agreement concluded between the host state and the international organisation before the latter is set up. Special provisions apply in Switzerland and the USA where such organisations are numerous.

## MEMBERS OF VISITING DIPLOMATIC MISSIONS

It is customary for states to grant privileges and immunities to visiting representatives of foreign states who, although not accredited as diplomats to any state, are exercising quasi-diplomatic or representative functions. Within this category come Heads of State or their representatives whether on a state occasion or on an informal visit, members of arbitration tribunals and government delegates to conferences or congresses. The New York Convention on Special Missions has now been drawn up to regulate the privileges and immunities given to such temporary special missions sent with the agreement of the receiving state.

# LIMITED PRIVILEGES AND IMMUNITIES

## NON-DIPLOMATIC STAFF OF A MISSION WHO ARE NOT NATIONALS OR PERMANENT RESIDENTS OF THE STATE IN WHICH THEY ARE SERVING

*Members of the administrative and technical staff* of a mission and members of their families forming part of their household (provided that they are not nationals or permanent residents of the state in which they are serving) are entitled to the full immunities given to a diplomat except that immunity from civil and administrative jurisdiction does not extend to acts performed outside the course of their duty; and to full diplomatic privileges except that they are not exempt from the inspection of their luggage, and exemption from customs duties is limited to articles imported at the time of their arrival in the state to take up their appointment there; nor are they entitled to privileges and immunities while travelling through third states to take up an appointment, though such states are obliged not to hinder their passage.

*Members of the domestic ('service') staff* of a mission who are not nationals or permanent residents of the state in which they are serving are entitled to immunity in respect of acts performed in the course of their duties, exemption from dues and taxes on the emoluments they receive in respect of their employment, and exemption from social security provisions in respect of their employment with a diplomatic mission provided that they are covered by the social security provisions of their own country.

*Private servants of members of the diplomatic staff* of a mission who are not nationals or permanent residents of the state in which they are serving are exempt from dues and taxes on the emoluments they receive in respect of their employment, but are not otherwise entitled to any privileges or immunities other than those that the host state may choose to grant; it is, however, bound to exercise its jurisdiction over them in such a manner as not to interfere unduly with the performance of the functions of the relevant mission.

## DIPLOMATS AND OTHER MEMBERS OF THE STAFF OF A MISSION WHO ARE NATIONALS OR PERMANENT RESIDENTS OF THE HOST STATE

Diplomats who are nationals or permanent residents of the state in which they are serving are entitled only to immunity from jurisdiction and personal inviolability in respect of official acts performed in the exercise of their functions, though other privileges and immunities may be granted in particular states. Other (non-diplomatic) members of the staff of a mission and private servants who are nationals or permanent residents of the state in which they are serving enjoy only those privileges and immunities that the host state considers appropriate. Any limitations placed on persons in these categories, however, must be such as not to interfere unduly with the performance of the functions of their mission.

Chapter 6

# CONSULAR OFFICERS AND CONSULAR POSTS

## THE ESTABLISHMENT OF CONSULAR POSTS

The establishment of diplomatic relations between states implies
agreement in principle to the establishment of consular relations
unless the contrary is specifically stated; but the severance of diplomatic relations does not automatically signify the severance of
consular relations.

The establishment of a consular post requires the prior approval
of the host state, which may ask to be provided with details
of the location and status of the post (i.e. Consulate-General,
Consulate, Vice-Consulate or Honorary Consulate) and its area
of consular jurisdiction. Its prior approval must also be obtained
for any subsequent changes in these particulars, and also for the
establishment of any subsidiary consular offices elsewhere in the
consular area.

## CONSULAR FUNCTIONS

Consular functions are described in general terms in the 1963 Vienna
Convention on Consular Relations as follows:

(a) protecting in the receiving state the interests of the sending
state and of its nationals, both individuals and bodies corporate,
within the limits permitted by international law;
(b) furthering the development of commercial, economic, cultural and
scientific relations between the sending state and the receiving

state and otherwise promoting friendly relations between them in accordance with the provisions of the Convention;

(c) ascertaining, by all lawful means, conditions and developments in the commercial, economic, cultural and scientific life of the receiving state, reporting thereon to the Government of the sending state and giving information to persons interested;

(d) issuing passports and travel documents to nationals of the sending state, and visas or appropriate documents to persons wishing to travel to the sending state;

(e) helping and assisting nationals, both individuals and bodies corporate, of the sending state;

(f) acting as notary and civil registrar and in capacities of a similar kind, and performing certain functions of an administrative nature, provided that there is nothing contrary thereto in the laws and regulations of the receiving state;

(g) safeguarding the interests of nationals, both individuals and bodies corporate, of the sending state in cases of succession *mortis causa* in the territory of the receiving state, in accordance with the laws and regulations of the receiving state;

(h) safeguarding, within the limits imposed by the laws and regulations of the receiving state, the interests of minors and other persons lacking full capacity who are nationals of the sending state, particularly where any guardianship or trusteeship is required with respect to such persons;

(i) subject to the practices and procedures in force in the receiving state, representing or arranging appropriate representation for nationals of the sending state before the tribunals and other authorities of the receiving state, for the purpose of obtaining, in accordance with the laws and regulations of the receiving state, provisional measures for the preservation of the rights and interests of these nationals, where, because of absence or any other reason, such nationals are unable at the proper time to assume the defence of their rights and interests;

(j) transmitting judicial and extra-judicial documents or executing letters rogatory or commissions to take evidence for the courts of the sending state in accordance with international agreements in force or, in the absence of such agreements, in any other manner compatible with the laws and regulations of the receiving state;

(k) exercising rights of supervision and inspection provided for in the laws and regulations of the sending state in respect of vessels having the nationality of the sending state, and of aircraft registered in that state, and in respect of their crews;

(l) extending assistance to vessels and aircraft mentioned in (k) above and to their crews, taking statements regarding the voyage of a vessel, examining and stamping the ship's papers, and without prejudice to the powers of the authorities of the receiving state, conducting investigations into any incidents which occurred during the voyage, and settling disputes of any kind between the master, the officers and the seamen in so far as this may be authorised by the laws and regulations of the sending state;

(m) performing any other functions entrusted to a consular post by the sending state which are not prohibited by the laws and regulations of the receiving state or to which no objection is taken by the receiving state or which are referred to in the international agreements in force between the sending state and the receiving state.

These functions may, with the consent of all governments concerned, be exercised by a consular officer on behalf of a third state.

It will be noted that in a substantial number of cases the right to act is not absolute, but dependent on the law of the receiving state. Also, despite the quasi-legal nature of many of his functions, a consul is not a substitute for a lawyer or other specialist.

More detailed provisions are included in many bilateral conventions, and a comprehensive outline of consular functions may be found in the Council of Europe, *European Convention on Consular Functions*.

A consular officer whose government has no diplomatic representative in the state in which he is serving and is not represented diplomatically by a third state may, with the authority of his host state, and without affecting his consular status, be authorised to perform certain diplomatic acts, including the representation of his state at intergovernmental organisations.

# CONSULAR OFFICERS, CONSULAR EMPLOYEES AND MEMBERS OF THE SERVICE STAFF

*Consular officers* are persons designated as such and responsible for the exercise of consular functions. They hold the rank of Consul-General, Consul or Vice-Consul and are divided into two categories:

(a) *career consular officers* who are full-time servants of their government and are appointed by their Head of State or Foreign Minister;

(b) *honorary consular officers* who are non-career officials for whom consular functions are usually a part-time occupation.

Career officers may not normally carry on for personal profit any professional or commercial activity in the host state, and should in principle have the nationality of the country they serve; the appointment of a national of the host state may only be made with that government's permission which may be withdrawn at any time. An honorary consular officer, on the other hand, though often a national of the country whose interest he serves, need not necessarily be so.

*Consular employees* are members of a consular staff who are not responsible for the exercise of consular functions but who are employed in an administrative or technical capacity.

*Members of the service staff* are those employed as chauffeurs, cleaners, domestics, etc. Persons falling within these categories are usually local residents.

*Consular agents and pro-consuls* are appointed by certain states but there is no standard definition of the terms. Generally they refer to consular employees with limited responsibilities ranking below vice-consul, but their precise status and functions vary considerably in different states.

# THE APPOINTMENT OF CONSULAR OFFICERS

It is traditional practice for the head of a consular post to be provided by his government with a written authority in respect of each appointment showing his full name, consular rank, consular district and post. This document (a *Commission*) is sent through diplomatic channels to the host government who, if they have no objection, issue a corresponding document (an *Exequatur*) authorising the appointment. In the rare event of its declining to issue an Exequatur, a government need give no reasons for its action. A similar procedure is normally adopted in respect of officers appointed to the consular staff; but, alternatively, a simple notification of relevant details in advance may be acceptable, and the granting of formal Exequaturs, though customary, is not obligatory.

The UK practice follows the Vienna Convention on Consular Relations, Article 12(1), whereby 'the Head of a Consular post is admitted to the exercise of his functions by an authorisation from the receiving State termed an exequatur whatever the form of this authorisation'. Pending the arrival of the officer's Commission, and on notification from the sending mission, the officer is granted the Secretary of State's Exequatur, thus enabling him to perform consular functions (Article 12(3)). If and when the officer's Commission is sent, the Queen's Exequatur is issued. This arrangement also applies to all officers performing consular functions.

On arrival at his post, the head of a consular post informs the Dean of the Consular Corps accordingly, and makes calls on the local authorities and on the other heads of consular posts.

As soon as a head of a consular post is admitted to his functions, and even though the formalities of his appointment may not have been completed, the host government notifies the official authorities in the consular district concerned and ensures that all necessary facilities are provided for him to carry out his functions. Customs and immigration authorities are also advised of the arrival and departure of a consular officer and members of his family so that appropriate arrangements can be made.

In the absence of the head of a consular post (whether through illness, or the post falling temporarily vacant) the position may be held provisionally by a diplomat or consular officer or, if the host state has no objection, by some other person. In any event the name of the acting head of post must be furnished to the host government, advance notification usually being required.

A consular officer may at any time and without explanation be declared *persona non grata*. In this event he is recalled by his government; failing which his Exequatur is cancelled and he ceases to be considered a consular officer.

# SEVERANCE OF CONSULAR RELATIONS

In the event of consular relations being broken off, the consular premises, property and archives must be respected and protected by the host state; and the business of the consulate, together with the property and archives, may be entrusted by the appointing state to a third state acceptable to the host state.

# PRIVILEGES, FACILITIES AND IMMUNITIES

The Vienna Convention on Consular Relations was drawn up in 1963 with the aim of providing the basis for a uniform practice in respect of consular privileges and immunities; but many states with wide consular interests have preferred to conclude bilateral agreements to suit their particular requirements, and these usually accord a more liberal scale of privileges, though not usually of immunities. Some states such as the United Kingdom are parties both to the Vienna Convention and to prior and subsequent bilateral Conventions. In case of any conflict they apply the more generous treatment in matters of privileges and immunities, on being assured of reciprocity. Nevertheless the advantages of a standard practice are self-evident and the following are the main provisions of the Vienna Convention.

# 1. CAREER CONSULAR OFFICERS AND POSTS HEADED BY THEM

## RELATING TO THE CONSULAR POST

The facilities granted by the host state to a consular post are those necessary to ensure the effective fulfilment of its functions: the premises used exclusively for consular purposes are (with minor exceptions such as an emergency requiring prompt action on the premises) inviolable and may not be entered except with the permission of the head of the consular post or the head of the diplomatic mission of the country concerned; the host state is obliged, where necessary, to help in the finding of suitable premises for the consular post (and accommodation for staff) and to ensure that all appropriate steps are taken to protect the premises from damage or insult; the consular archives and official correspondence are inviolable; there is freedom of movement for members of the post (save in generally restricted zones) and freedom and inviolability of communication by bag and other recognised means, although wireless transmitters may be used only with the permission of the host government; furthermore the host government may ask for a bag to be opened if it has serious reason to believe that its contents are unauthorised (if, however, the sending state refuses to do this the bag shall be returned to its place of origin); and the head of post has the right to fly his national flag and display his national coat of arms on his premises and residence, and fly his flag on his car, boat or aircraft when on official business.

The consular premises, including the residence of the head of the post but not those of other members of the staff, are not directly liable to taxation (though this exemption does not apply to the vendor or lessor of the premises if he is liable under the law), but charges for services, e.g. refuse collection, must be met.

In addition, consular fees and charges may be levied for services rendered, e.g. the granting of visas, certification of documents; these are exempt from all dues and taxes in the host state.

## RELATING TO CONSULAR DUTIES

### *Right of access to nationals who are detained*
In view of a consular officer's particular responsibility within his consular district towards nationals of his own state (and those of any other state or states whose interests he represents) he must be free to visit and communicate with them; and such individuals, conversely, have the right to communicate with and have free access to their consular officer. Moreover, if the authorities detain a foreign national they must inform him that he is free to communicate with his consular officer, who must be given the appropriate facilities to visit the national if the latter so wishes. If a consular officer makes enquiries as to whether an individual for whom he is responsible has been detained, he must be given an immediate reply and be permitted, where he considers it necessary and with the concurrence of the person concerned, to arrange for appropriate legal representation.

### *Right of access to information in cases of death, guardianship or trusteeship, wrecks and air accidents*
The appropriate authorities have the duty to notify a consular officer without delay of any incident of which they are aware occurring within his district and affecting individuals for whom he is responsible, such as a death, a case where the appointment of guardians or trustees is needed, or a wreck or accident occurring to a ship or aircraft registered in his state.

### *Right of access to appropriate authorities*
In the exercise of his official functions a consular officer is entitled to communicate with the competent local authorities in his consular area; and in exceptional cases with the central authorities if custom and circumstances permit.

## PERSONAL PRIVILEGES AND IMMUNITIES

### *General*
The privileges to which a career consular officer is entitled under the 1963 Vienna Convention on Consular Relations are similar to those of members of the diplomatic staff of a mission. The extent of his immunity from jurisdiction and personal inviolability,

however, is considerably less except where specific agreements provide otherwise. Privileges and immunities apply from the moment he enters the host state to take up his appointment or, if already in the country, from the moment he takes up his duties. They terminate when he leaves the country or (if he does not leave immediately) a reasonable time after he relinquishes his appointment.

*Personal protection*
The host state is obliged to treat a consular officer with due respect and must take all appropriate steps to prevent any attack on his person, freedom or dignity.

*Personal inviolability and immunity from jurisdiction*
A consular officer or consular employee is not liable to the jurisdiction (judicial or administrative) of the host state in respect of acts performed in the exercise of his consular functions. It is expressly made clear that his immunity does not apply to civil actions by third parties, (i) for damage arising within the state from an accident caused by a vehicle, vessel or aircraft or (ii) arising out of any contract that he concluded if he did not contract expressly or impliedly as an agent of the state which he was serving at the time. His government may, if it sees fit, waive his immunity.

He must, however, appear before the competent authorities if criminal proceedings are brought against him, and he is liable to imprisonment if convicted by the competent judicial authorities. In the event of his being accused of a grave crime (but only in such an event) he may be detained pending trial.

It is, nevertheless, some consolation for him to know that proceedings will be carried out with the minimum delay, with due respect to him by reason of his official position, and, if the charge is not serious, with the minimum interference to his consular functions; and that the head of his consular post must be informed of his predicament unless he himself holds that position, in which case his government will be informed immediately through diplomatic channels.

*Proceedings initiated by a consular officer or consular employee*
If a consular officer or consular employee initiates proceedings, he loses any immunity from jurisdiction in respect of any counterclaim directly connected with the main claim to which he would otherwise have been entitled.

*Liability to give evidence*
No member of a consular post is obliged (unless his government waives the immunity) to give evidence on official matters or to

produce official correspondence and documents concerning matters connected with the exercise of his functions; nor is he bound to give evidence as an expert witness with regard to the law of his state. In other matters he may be called on to attend as a witness at judicial or administrative proceedings and would normally do so. If a consular officer (as opposed to a consular employee or member of the service staff) should decline to do so, however, no penalty or coercive measure may be applied to him.

## Residence permits, work permits, and registration as aliens

Career consular officers, consular employees (provided that they are permanent employees of the state they serve and are not engaged in any gainful occupation in the state in which they are serving) and members of their families forming part of their household are exempt from local regulations concerning residence permits, the registration of aliens and the employment of aliens.

## Social security

Career consular officers and other members of the consular post (i.e. consular employees and members of the service staff) together with members of their families forming part of their household are exempt from social security requirements in force in the host state in respect of their official duties. They may, however, be permitted to participate voluntarily; and if they have any individuals in their private employ, they are responsible for complying with the social security requirements in respect of such persons.

## Taxation

Career consular officers and consular employees and members of their families forming part of their household, provided that they do not carry on any private gainful occupation in the host state, are exempt from all national and local taxes, except:

(a) indirect taxes of a kind normally incorporated in the price of goods or services;

(b) dues or taxes on private immovable property in the territory of the host state (this provision does not apply to the premises of a career consular post or to the residence of the head of such post);

(c) estate, succession or inheritance duties and duties on transfers levied by the host state (this provision does not normally apply to movable property of a deceased person which is sent out of the country);

(d) dues and taxes on private income (including capital gains) originating in the host state, and capital taxes on investments in commercial or financial undertakings in the host state;

(e) charges levied for specific services rendered;
(f) registration, court or record fees, mortgage dues and stamp duties (this provision does not apply to the premises of a career consular post or to the residence of the head of such post).

Members of the service staff are exempt from dues and taxes on the wages that they receive for their services.

*Customs duties and inspection*
Exemption from all customs duties, taxes and related charges (other than those for storage, cartage, etc.) and unrestricted right of entry (except for articles generally restricted by law) are granted in respect of:

(a) articles for the official use of the *consular post*.
(b) articles for the personal and domestic use of a *consular officer* and members of his family (forming part of his household) in reasonable quantities;
(c) articles for the personal and domestic use of a *consular employee* and members of his family (forming part of his household) imported at the time of his first arrival to take up his duties.

*Insurance against third-party risks*
All members of a consular post must comply with national and local legislation concerning third party insurance in respect of any vehicle, vessel or aircraft.

# 2. HONORARY CONSULAR OFFICERS AND POSTS HEADED BY THEM

## RELATING TO THE CONSULAR POST

A certain number of the facilities and immunities granted to career posts (with the same provisos as to their use exclusively for consular functions) are granted to consular posts headed by honorary consuls:

(a) full facilities for the performance of the functions of a consular post;
(b) the right to display the national flag and emblem at the consular post and consular residence and on a vehicle when on official business;
(c) assistance in the acquisition of premises and accommodation;
(d) freedom of movement and travel of all members of the consular post (save in generally restricted areas);

(e) freedom and inviolability of communication (including the right of communication through third states); but the exchange of consular bags between two consular posts headed by honorary consular officers in different states is not permitted without the consent of the two host states concerned;

(f) the right to levy consular fees and charges, and their exemption from taxation in the host state;

(g) more limited protection by the host state of the consular premises against intrusion, damage, disturbance and impairment of its dignity;

(h) exemption from all forms of taxation of the consular premises of which the sending state is owner or lessee except for those representing the payment for specific services rendered: but this exemption does not extend to the individual who leases or sells the premises to the sending state if he is liable to pay under the law;

(i) inviolability of consular archives and documents at all times and wherever they may be, provided that they are kept separate from other papers and documents and, in particular, from the private correspondence of the head of a consular post and of any person working with him, and from the materials, books or documents relating to their profession or trade;

(j) exemption from customs and other similar duties on coats-of-arms, flags, signboards, seals and stamps, books, official printed matter, office furniture, office equipment and similar articles supplied by or at the instance of the sending state to the consular post provided that they are for official use.

## RELATING TO CONSULAR DUTIES

(a) the right of access to nationals for whom the post is responsible;

(b) the right of access to information in cases of deaths, the need for guardianships or trusteeships, wrecks and air accidents;

(c) the right of access to the appropriate authorities in the host state.

## FACILITIES, PERSONAL PRIVILEGES AND IMMUNITIES

An honorary consular officer enjoys a certain number of the facilities, privileges and immunities enjoyed by a career consular officer in connection with the performance of his functions, though, as with career officers, they may be waived by the government he serves; and if he himself initiates legal proceedings he loses the immunity (see below) in respect of a counterclaim directly connected with a principal claim.

They start the moment the officer enters the territory of the state to take up his post, or if he is already in the territory, the moment that he takes up his duties, and come to an end when he leaves the territory or (if he does not do so immediately) a reasonable period thereafter.

These facilities, privileges and immunities are as follows:

(a) The obligation of the host state to notify his consular or diplomatic representative in the event of his being arrested, detained or prosecuted.

(b) Immunity from jurisdiction in respect of acts performed in the exercise of his consular functions except for civil actions (i) in respect of third-party claims arising from an accident caused by a vehicle, vessel or aircraft, or (ii) arising out of a contract not expressly or impliedly carried out as an agent of the state which he, as an honorary consular officer, serves. The immunity is of indefinite duration, i.e. it does not necessarily cease on the termination of the officer's period of duty.

(c) Freedom from the obligation to give evidence or to produce official correspondence or documents on matters connected with the exercise of his consular functions; and the right to decline to give evidence as an expert witness with regard to the law of the state he serves.

The following additional provisions also apply to an honorary consular officer:

(d) If criminal proceedings are instituted against him he must appear before the competent authorities. He is, however, treated with the respect due to his official position; proceedings are instituted with the minimum of delay; and unless under detention, his ability to carry on his consular functions is hampered as little as possible.

(e) He is exempt from all obligations in the host state in regard to the registration of aliens and residence permits provided that he does not engage there in any professional or commercial activity for personal profit.

(f) He is exempt from all dues and taxes on the remuneration and emoluments that he receives from the government of the state he serves in respect of the exercise of his consular functions.

(g) He is exempt from all personal and public services and military contributions in the state in which he is serving.

(h) He is entitled to receive from the host state such protection as is needed on account of his official position; and in return must undertake to respect the laws of that state and not to interfere in its internal affairs.

(i) Privileges and immunities granted to an honorary consular officer do not apply to members of his family, nor to the family of a consular employee in a post headed by an honorary consul.

# Chapter 7

# THE UNITED NATIONS

## PURPOSES AND PRINCIPLES

The United Nations has been aptly described as a Standing Diplomatic Conference: it is a worldwide association of states which, on signing the Charter of the United Nations, subscribe to its purposes and agree to act in accordance with its principles; these are:

### PURPOSES

I    To maintain international peace and security, and to that end: to take effective collective measures for the prevention and removal of threats to the peace, and for the suppression of acts of aggression or other breaches of the peace, and to bring about by peaceful means, and in conformity with the principles of justice and international law, adjustment or settlement of international disputes or situations which might lead to a breach of the peace;

II   To develop friendly relations among nations based on respect for the principle of equal rights and self-determination of peoples, and to take other appropriate measures to strengthen universal peace;

III  To achieve international cooperation in solving international problems of an economic, social, cultural, or humanitarian character, and in promoting and encouraging respect for human rights and for fundamental freedoms for all without distinction as to race, sex, language, or religion; and

IV   To be a centre for harmonising the actions of nations in the attainment of these common ends.

## PRINCIPLES

I  The United Nations is based on the principle of the sovereign equality of all its members.

II  All members, in order to ensure to all of them the rights and benefits resulting from membership, shall fulfil in good faith the obligations assumed by them in accordance with the Charter.

III  All members shall settle their international disputes by peaceful means in such a manner that international peace and security, and justice, are not endangered.

IV  All members shall refrain in their international relations from the threat or use of force against the territorial integrity or political independence of any state, or in any other manner inconsistent with the Purposes of the United Nations.

V  All members shall give the United Nations every assistance in any action it takes in accordance with the Charter, and shall refrain from giving assistance to any state against which the United Nations is taking a preventive or enforcement action.

VI  The United Nations shall ensure that states which are not members of the Organisation act in accordance with these Principles so far as may be necessary for the maintenance of international peace and security.

VII  Nothing contained in the Charter shall authorise the United Nations to intervene in matters which are essentially within the domestic jurisdiction of any state or shall require the members to submit such matters to settlement under the Charter; but this principle shall not prejudice the application of enforcement measures under chapter VII.

# THE UNITED NATIONS CHARTER

The Charter is divided into 111 articles grouped in nineteen chapters:

<table>
<tr><td>I</td><td>Purposes and Principles</td><td>(articles 1 and 2)</td></tr>
<tr><td>II</td><td>Membership</td><td>(articles 3–6)</td></tr>
<tr><td>III</td><td>Organs</td><td>(articles 7 and 8)</td></tr>
<tr><td>IV</td><td>The General Assembly</td><td></td></tr>
<tr><td></td><td>Composition</td><td>(article 9)</td></tr>
<tr><td></td><td>Functions and powers</td><td>(articles 10–17)</td></tr>
<tr><td></td><td>Voting</td><td>(articles 18 and 19)</td></tr>
<tr><td></td><td>Procedure</td><td>(articles 20–22)</td></tr>
</table>

Membership of the United Nations consists of the 'original members' (those states which signed the Washington Declaration in 1942 or took part in the United Nations Conference on International Organisation in San Francisco in 1945, and signed and ratified the Charter in accordance with the prescribed procedure); and those states subsequently accepted as members in accordance with the provisions of the Charter.

Membership is further open to all other 'peace-loving' states which accept the obligations contained in the Charter and, in the judgement of the United Nations, are able and willing to carry them out. The admission of new members is dependent on the approval of the General Assembly on the recommendation of the Security Council.

A member which has persistently violated the principles of the Charter may be expelled from the United Nations by the General

Assembly on the recommendation of the Security Council; or may
have its rights and privileges of membership suspended by the
General Assembly on the recommendation of the Security Council
if it has been the object of preventive or enforcement action taken
by the Security Council. These rights and privileges, however, may
be restored by the Security Council.

Each state is entitled to one vote in the General Assembly and in
its dependent committees and councils.

Provision is made in chapter XVIII for amendments to the Charter, and these come into force when they have been (a) adopted
by a vote of two-thirds of the members of the General Assembly,
and (b) ratified in accordance with their respective constitutional
processes by two-thirds of the members of the Security Council. The
procedure is the same if a General Conference of the members of the
United Nations is convened in terms of article 109 for the purpose
of reviewing the Charter, except that the requirement for the initial
vote (prior to ratification) is a two-thirds majority of those present
at the Conference.

The official languages of the United Nations are Arabic, Chinese,
English, French, Russian and Spanish.

The United Nations, in terms of its Charter, is based on six
principal organs: the General Assembly, the Security Council, the
Economic and Social Council, the Trusteeship Council, the International Court of Justice, and the Secretariat. Generally speaking
the Assembly and Security Council are the political and legislative
bodies, ECOSOC and the Trusteeship Council are specialist bodies
dependent on the General Assembly, and the International Court of
Justice an independent body.

# THE GENERAL ASSEMBLY

The General Assembly consists of all members of the United
Nations. In terms of the Charter, the United Nations may not
intervene in matters which are essentially within the jurisdiction of
a state, except in respect of the application of enforcement measures
in accordance with chapter VII (threats to the peace, breaches of the
peace and acts of aggression). Subject to this proviso, the functions
of the Assembly are:

*To consider and discuss* (i) any matter within the scope of the Charter
or relating to the powers and functions of any of the organs
provided for in the Charter, (ii) general principles of cooperation
in the maintenance of international peace and security, including

principles governing disarmament and the regulation of armaments, and (iii) any question relating to the maintenance of
international peace and security.

*To call the attention* of the Security Council to situations which are
likely to endanger international peace and security.

*To make recommendations* to the Security Council or to member
states (or both) or to a non-member state involved in questions
relating to the maintenance of international peace and security
in respect of (ii) and (iii) above; for the purpose of promoting
international cooperation in the political field and encouraging the
progressive development of international law and its codification;
and for promoting international cooperation in the economic,
social, cultural, educational and health fields, and assisting in
the realisation of human rights and fundamental freedoms for all
without distinction as to race, sex, language or religion.

*To make recommendations – subject to the proviso* that if the Security
Council is already exercising its prescribed function in respect of
such matters, recommendations will only be made if asked for –
relating to:

(a) any matter within the scope of the Charter or relating to the
powers and functions of any of the organs provided for in the
Charter;

(b) the peaceful adjustment of any situation, regardless of origin,
which it deems likely to impair the general welfare or friendly
relations among nations, including situations resulting from a
violation of the provisions of the Charter setting forth the
Purposes and Principles of the United Nations.

*To receive and consider annual and special reports* from the Security
Council (including an account of the measures that it has decided
upon or taken to maintain international peace and security), and
from the other organs of the United Nations.

*To perform such functions* with respect to the international trusteeship system as are assigned to it under chapters XII and XIII,
including the approval of the trusteeship agreements for areas not
designated as strategic.

*To consider and approve* the United Nations budget and any financial
and budgetary arrangements with the Specialised Agencies and to
examine the administrative budgets of such Specialised Agencies
with a view to making recommendations to the Agencies concerned.

In the event of a non-member state being involved in a question
relating to the maintenance of international peace and security, the
Assembly may make recommendations to the state concerned; and

any question on which action is necessary in such circumstances shall be referred to the Security Council by the Assembly either before or after discussion.

The regular sessions of the Assembly as a rule begin in New York on the third Tuesday in September each year and continue until mid-December, but special sessions may be called by the Secretary-General at the request of the Security Council or of a majority of the members of the United Nations. At the start of each regular session, the Assembly elects a new President, twenty-one Vice-Presidents and the Chairman of the Assembly's seven Main Committees. To ensure equitable geographical representation, the Presidency of the Assembly rotates each year among five groups of States – African, Asian, Eastern European, Latin American, and Western European and Other States.

The work of the General Assembly is coordinated and to a considerable extent organised by two procedural committees: the *General Committee*, which is made up of the President and Vice-Presidents of the General Assembly and the heads of the seven *Main Committees* and the *Credentials Committee*.

The *Main Committees*, which consider in advance matters placed on the agenda of the General Assembly and (when so requested) make recommendations for consideration by the Assembly in plenary session, are:

First Committee: Disarmament and related international security
    matters
Special Political Committee
Second Committee: Economic and Financial
Third Committee: Social, Humanitarian and Cultural
Fourth Committee: Trusteeship and non-self-governing territories
Fifth Committee: Administrative and Budgetary
Sixth Committee: Legal

The Special Political Committee was created primarily to relieve the First Committee; and there are two *Standing Committees*: the Committee on Contributions, and the Advisory Committee on Administrative and Budgetary Questions. Subsidiary and *ad hoc* committees are set up from time to time to deal with specific problems.

Voting in the Assembly is by simple majority of the members present and voting; except in the following circumstances, when the necessary majority is the affirmative vote of two-thirds of the members present and voting:

• recommendations with respect to the maintenance of international peace and security,

- the election of non-permanent members of the Security Council,
- the election of members of the Economic and Social Council,
- the election of members of the Trusteeship Council,
- the admission of new members to the United Nations,
- the suspension of the rights and privileges of members,
- the expulsion of members,
- matters relating to the operation of the trusteeship system,
- budgetary questions,
- any other matters considered by the Assembly (by a simple majority of the members present and voting) to be sufficiently important to require a two-thirds majority

A member in arrears in the payment of its financial contributions to the United Nations is not entitled to vote if its arrears equal or exceed the amount of its contributions due for the preceding two full years, unless the General Assembly is satisfied that failure to pay is due to circumstances beyond the member's control.

Much of the work of the United Nations is conducted on the basis of regional groups: e.g. African States, Asian States, Latin American States and Western European and Other States. For election purposes the USA falls within Western European and Other States.

# THE SECURITY COUNCIL

The Security Council consists of fifteen members: China, France, Russia, the United Kingdom and the USA, who constitute the five permanent members; and ten non-permanent members elected by the General Assembly for a term of two years (provided that no member is elected for two consecutive periods). So that it may function continuously, a representative of each of its members must be present at all times at the United Nations Headquarters. It has primary responsibility for the maintenance of international peace and security, and for this purpose acts on behalf of the members of the United Nations and in accordance with its purposes and principles. The members of the United Nations, for their part, agree to accept and carry out the decisions of the Security Council in accordance with the Charter.

The powers of the Security Council are specified in chapters VI and VII of the Charter. In terms of chapter VI the Council may investigate any dispute or situation which is referred to it by a state or which it considers may lead to international friction; and if it determines that its continuation is likely to endanger the maintenance of international peace and security it will try to resolve it by peaceful settlement.

If it determines the existence of any threat to the peace, breach of the peace or act of aggression, the Security Council is empowered in terms of chapter VII to decide what measures shall be taken to maintain or restore international peace and security; these may take the form of non-violent measures or, if they fail, the use of force by land, sea or air. The provision of armed forces by member states is governed by article 43 of the Charter, and is subject to special agreements requiring ratification between such states and the Security Council.

The Security Council is required to submit annual and, where necessary, special reports to the General Assembly for its consideration, including plans for the establishment of whatever subsidiary organs it may consider necessary for the performance of its functions (e.g. the United Nations Truce Supervision Organisation in Palestine).

The General Assembly or any member state (or a non-member state under certain conditions) may bring to the attention of the Security Council any dispute or situation likely to endanger international peace and security.

Any state, whether it is a member of the United Nations or not, which is a party to a dispute under consideration by the Security Council and is not itself a member of the Council, has the right to participate (but not vote) in the deliberations. Similar provisions apply to any member state which, not being a party to a dispute nor a member of the Security Council, is nevertheless considered by the Council to be affected by the dispute.

In terms of articles 27 and 109(1) of the Charter (as amended), decisions of the Security Council require the affirmative votes of nine members *including the concurring votes of the permanent members*; except (a) on procedural matters and (b) for deciding to hold and for fixing a date and place for a Conference to review the Charter, when the affirmative votes of *any* nine members suffice. Abstentions have not, in practice, always been interpreted in terms of the Charter. Amendments to the Charter require to be ratified by all the permanent members of the Council.

In decisions under chapter VI (pacific settlement of disputes) and article 52, para 3 (the pacific settlement of local disputes through regional arrangements) any member of the Security Council who is a party to a dispute is required to abstain from voting.

Dependent bodies of the Security Council are, for example the United Nations Disengagement Observer Force (UNDOF); the

United Nations Peace-keeping Force in Cyprus (UNFICYP) and the United Nations Interim Force in Lebanon (UNIFIL).

# THE ECONOMIC AND SOCIAL COUNCIL

ECOSOC consists of fifty-four members elected by the General Assembly, and is responsible under the Assembly and in conjunction with the Specialised Agencies and other governmental and non-governmental international organisations for promoting:

(a) higher standards of living, full employment, and conditions of economic and social progress and development;
(b) solutions of international economic, social, health, and related problems; and international cultural and educational cooperation;
(c) universal respect for, and observance of, human rights and fundamental freedoms for all without distinction as to race, sex, language or religion.

The Council meets twice a year: in New York in April and in Geneva in July. Decisions in the Council are reached on a simple majority of those members present and voting.

ECOSOC functions on the basis of seven *standing committees*, seven *standing expert bodies*, six *functional commissions* and five *regional commissions*; as well as various *ad hoc* expert bodies.

The *standing committees* are on Non-Governmental Organisations; Negotiations with Intergovernmental Agencies; Housing, Building and Planning; Programme and Coordination; Natural Resources; and the Commissions on Transnational Corporations and on Human Settlements.

The *standing expert bodies* are on crime prevention and control; development planning; the application of science and technology to development; tax reform planning; tax treaties between developed and developing countries; the UN programme in public administration; and the transport of dangerous goods.

The *functional commissions* are:

Commission on Statistics
Commission on Human Rights (including the Sub-Commission on the Prevention of Discrimination and Protection of Minorities)
Commission for Social Development
Commission on the Status of Women
Commission on Narcotic Drugs
Population Commission

The *regional commissions*, which act on behalf of the United Nations in all social and economic matters are:

Economic Commission for Europe (Geneva)
Economic and Social Commission for Asia and the Pacific (Bangkok)
Economic Commission for Latin America and the Caribbean, (Santiago, Chile)
Economic Commission for Africa (Addis Ababa)
Economic and Social Commission for Western Asia (Baghdad)

# THE TRUSTEESHIP COUNCIL

The Trusteeship system was established under the authority of the United Nations for the administration and supervision of certain territories falling within the categories defined in article 77 of the Charter and placed under trusteeship by means of individual agreements with the states directly concerned (including mandatory powers where such already existed). The agreements require the approval of the General Assembly, and the principles of trusteeship are defined in article 76. Eleven territories have been placed under United Nations' Trusteeship; ten have achieved independent status and the remaining one, Palau in the South Pacific administered by the USA, is in the process of achieving self-government. Trust territories are directly controlled by the administering states in terms of their particular Trusteeship Agreement.

The Council, now that its work is almost completed, consists only of the administering state (the USA) and the remaining permanent members of the Security Council: China, France, Russia and the UK. It meets annually in New York, receives reports from the administering state, accepts petitions and makes periodic visits of inspection.

# THE INTERNATIONAL COURT OF JUSTICE

The International Court of Justice is situated at The Hague and is the principal judicial organ of the United Nations. It functions in accordance with the provisions of its Statute to which all members of the United Nations automatically subscribe. The Court is composed of fifteen suitably qualified judges elected by secret ballot by the General Assembly and by the Security Council (independently) for a term of nine years. They retire in groups of five every three years (their re-election is permitted); and no two judges may be nationals of the same state.

Access to the Court is open to states which subscribe to its statute, and to non-subscribing states under certain conditions. The functions of the Court are twofold: to give judgment on all contentious cases referred to it by states by mutual consent, and on all matters specially provided for in the United Nations Charter, in treaties or in conventions; and to give advisory opinions in legal questions referred to it by any branch of the United Nations or its Agencies. The Court will normally base its decisions on International Law, but it may also reach a decision, if both parties agree, *ex aequo et bono*, i.e. on general principles of fairness and natural justice.

A state may at any time lodge a declaration to the effect that it recognises as compulsory, in relation to any other state accepting the same obligation, the jurisdiction of the Court in certain specific instances. These are listed in article 36(2) of the Statute (the so-called 'Optional Clause'), namely:

(a) the interpretation of a treaty;
(b) any question of international law;
(c) the existence of any fact which, if established, would constitute a breach of an international obligation;
(d) the nature or extent of the reparation to be made for the breach of an international obligation.

The declaration may be made unconditionally; on condition of reciprocity on the part of several or certain states; or for a certain time. In practice the forty-seven states that have lodged declarations in terms of article 36 have tended to add other provisos.

The official languages of the Court are English and French, but the Court is bound to allow a party to use whatever language it chooses. The procedure consists of two parts: written and oral, and the hearings in Court are public unless the Court decides otherwise or the parties concerned so desire. All questions are decided by a majority vote of the judges present, and in the event of an equality of votes the President or the judge who acts in his place has a casting (i.e. deciding) vote. A judgment is final and without appeal, though the court may subsequently recognise the discovery of fresh evidence of a decisive nature, and permit an application for a revision of a judgment to proceed. Since its inception, the Court has delivered fifty-four judgments in addition to advisory opinions.

# THE SECRETARY-GENERAL AND THE SECRETARIAT

In terms of the United Nations Charter the Secretary-General is the chief administrative officer of the Organisation. He acts as such at all meetings of the General Assembly, the Security Council and the Trusteeship Council, and carries out whatever functions these bodies assign to him. He submits an annual report to the General Assembly on the work of the Organisation, and may bring to the attention of the Security Council any matter which in his opinion may threaten the maintenance of international peace and security. He is appointed by the General Assembly on the recommendation of the Security Council for a period of five years, and he is responsible for the appointment of the staff of the Organisation in accordance with the regulations drawn up by the General Assembly. Selection of staff is primarily on the basis of merit, but representation on a balanced geographical basis is also a relevant factor. The Secretary-General and his staff are bound to act as international civil servants and may not seek or receive instructions from any government, or from any authority outside the Organisation; and member states similarly undertake not to try to influence them in any way.

# INTERGOVERNMENTAL AGENCIES RELATED TO THE UNITED NATIONS (INCLUDING SPECIALISED AGENCIES)

The intergovernmental agencies related to the United Nations by special agreements are separate, autonomous organisations which work with the United Nations and each other through the co-ordinating machinery of the Economic and Social Council. Sixteen of the agencies are known as specialised agencies, a term used in the United Nations Charter. They report annually to the Economic and Social Council. The International Atomic Energy Agency (IAEA), established in 1957 under the aegis of the United Nations, reports annually to the General Assembly and, as appropriate, to the Security Council and the Economic and Social Council. The General Agreement on Tariffs and Trade (GATT) is a multilateral agreement which provides a forum for negotiation and lays down rules for international trade.

## INTERNATIONAL ATOMIC ENERGY AGENCY

The IAEA encourages and coordinates research into the peaceful uses of atomic energy. It advises members on such subjects as the development of nuclear power, the uses of radioactive material in the fields of medicine, agriculture, etc., the disposal of radioactive waste, and water desalination; it provides experts where necessary, and offers research fellowships and training facilities.

In addition to its purely technical role the IAEA has increased responsibility under the 1968 Treaty of the Non-proliferation of Nuclear Weapons for ensuring adequate safeguards and preventing the diversion of nuclear energy from peaceful uses to nuclear weapons in those non-nuclear states which are signatories of the treaty.

It is also responsible for implementing the International Nuclear Information System (INIS) which collects and disseminates information relating to nuclear matters. There are 113 members of the Agency, including Argentina, Belarus, China, France, India, Iraq, Israel, Pakistan, Russia, UK, Ukraine and the USA.

The headquarters of the Agency is at the UN City in Vienna, and it is controlled by an annual Conference of member states and a Board of Governors of thirty-four.


## INTERNATIONAL LABOUR ORGANISATION

The ILO was founded in 1919 and seeks to raise the standards and dignity of human labour throughout the world. It formulates conventions, makes recommendations, receives reports on labour conditions and related matters, and undertakes research and enquiries. It has its headquarters and secretariat (the International Labour Office) in Geneva, regional offices in Addis Ababa, Bangkok, Istanbul and Lima, and an International Centre for Advanced Technical and Vocational Training in Turin. Policy is determined by a Conference of all members which meets annually, member states being represented by two government delegates, one employers' delegate and one employees' delegate, and decisions being on the basis of a two-thirds majority. The executive of the organisation is the fifty-six-member Governing Body which meets quarterly and is responsible for determining programmes, convening conferences, preparing the budget and appointing the Director-General. It is part-nominated and part-elected by the Conference, and consists of twenty-eight government members, fourteen employers' members and fourteen employees' members.

## FOOD AND AGRICULTURE ORGANISATION

The FAO has extensive functions covering all aspects of food production and related activities. It collects, reviews, and makes available information and statistics on world agriculture, forestry and fisheries; it includes within its scope production, trade, consumption, nutrition, marketing, land tenure, and the protection of natural resources. It arranges for the provision of technical experts, assists in the negotiation of commodity and other related agreements, and is the coordinating body for the World Food Programme. The Director-General and Secretariat are in Rome, and there are regional offices in Accra, Addis Ababa, Bangkok, Santiago and Cairo, and liaison offices in Washington and New York. Policy is determined by a Conference of representatives of all member countries which meets every two years and on which each member state is represented; responsibility in the period between its sessions rests with a Council of forty-nine elected by the Conference.

## UNITED NATIONS EDUCATIONAL, SCIENTIFIC AND CULTURAL ORGANISATION

The aims of UNESCO are concentrated on practical projects for raising educational standards throughout the world; the exchange of knowledge; and the encouragement of international cooperation in the fields of education, science and culture. It seeks to provide better living conditions through scientific research and cooperation and to improve the scope and quality of mass communications throughout the world. It has its headquarters and Secretariat in Paris, and is controlled by a General Conference of all member states meeting every two years and an Executive Board of fifty-one meeting at least three times a year. National commissions extend the sphere of UNESCO activities to include the majority of member countries, and there are branch offices in New York and Havana; regional education offices in Santiago, Bangkok, Dakar and Beirut; and regional science offices in Nairobi, Montevideo, Cairo, Delhi and Jakarta.

## WORLD HEALTH ORGANISATION

The aim of the WHO is the improvement of world standards of health – principally physical, but also mental and social. In view of the extent and diversity of the problems it has to face it has established regional offices in Alexandria, Brazzaville, Copenhagen,

Delhi, Manila and Washington, and committees of experts in a wide number of fields. It has its headquarters and Secretariat in Geneva and is controlled by the World Health Assembly consisting of all member states meeting annually and an Executive Board of thirty-one elected by the Assembly.

## THE WORLD BANK AND IFC

The expression 'The World Bank' means both the International Bank for Reconstruction and Development (IBRD) and its affiliate, the International Development Association (IDA). The IBRD has a second affiliate, the International Finance Corporation (IFC). The common objective of these institutions is to help raise standards of living in developing countries by channelling financial resources from developed countries to the developing world. The Board of Governors consists of twelve members from developing countries and twelve from donor countries; voting being weighted, with the USA having the principal voting rights.

*The IBRD* was established in 1945. Its capital is subscribed by its member countries, and it finances its lending operations primarily from its own borrowing in the world capital markets. A substantial contribution to the IBRD's resources also comes from its retained earnings and the flow of repayments on its loans. These generally have a grace period of five years and are repayable over twenty years or less. They are directed towards developing countries at more advanced stages of economic and social growth. The interest rate the IBRD charges on its loans is calculated in accordance with a guideline related to its cost of borrowing. The IBRD's Charter spells out certain basic rules that govern its operations. It must lend only for productive purposes, and must stimulate economic growth in the developing countries where it lends. It must pay due regard to the prospects of repayment, and each loan is made to a government or must be guaranteed by the government concerned. The use of loans cannot be restricted to purchases in any particular member country, and the IBRD's decision to lend must be based on economic considerations.

*The International Development Association* was established in 1960 to provide assistance for the same purposes as the IBRD, but primarily to the lower-income developing countries and on terms that would bear less heavily on their balance of payments than IBRD loans. IDA's assistance is, therefore, concentrated on the lowest-income group of countries. More than fifty countries are eligible under this criterion. Membership of IDA is open to all members of the IBRD. The funds used by IDA, called 'credits' in order to distinguish them from IBRD loans, come mostly in the form of subscriptions, general replenishments from IDA's more industrialised and developed members, and transfers from the net earnings of the IBRD. The terms of IDA credits, which are made to governments only, are ten-year grace periods, fifty-year maturities, and no interest.

*The IFC* was established in 1956. Its function is to assist the economic development of less-developed countries by promoting growth in the private sector of their economies and helping to mobilise domestic and foreign capital for this purpose. Membership in the IBRD is a prerequisite for membership of the IFC. Legally and financially, the IFC and the IBRD are separate entities. The IFC has its own operating and legal staff, but draws upon the Bank for administrative and other services.

While the World Bank has traditionally financed all kinds of capital infrastructure such as roads and railways, telecommunications, and ports and power facilities, its development strategy also places an emphasis on investments that can directly affect the well-being of the masses of poor people of developing countries by making them more productive and by integrating them as active partners in the development process.

In 1980, the Bank, in response to the deteriorated prospects for the developing countries, inaugurated a programme of *structural adjustment loans* (SALS). This lending supports programmes of specific policy changes and institutional reforms in developing countries designed to achieve a more efficient use of resources, thereby: (a) contributing to a more sustainable balance of payments in the medium and long term and to the maintenance of growth in the face of severe constraints; and (b) laying the basis for regaining momentum for future growth. At the same time it introduced *sector adjustment loans* (SECALS) in order to promote economic reform within a specific sector such as agricultural price reform.

## THE INTERNATIONAL MONETARY FUND

The International Monetary Fund is an intergovernmental organisation based on a treaty drafted at Bretton Woods, New Hampshire, in 1944 (amended in 1969 and in 1978), and membership of the Fund is a prerequisite of membership of the World Bank.

The essential purpose of the Fund is to promote international monetary cooperation and thereby foster expanded international trade. It is a permanent forum where countries can work to co-ordinate their economic and financial policies, and is concerned not only with the problems of individual countries but also with the working of the international monetary system. As the world monetary system has changed, so too has the Fund, but the underlying purposes of the organisation and of membership in it remain the same. It has both regulatory and financing functions.

Members agree to abide by a code of economic behaviour and to cooperate with the Fund and with each other to ensure orderly exchange arrangements, to promote exchange stability and to avoid restrictions that would harm national and international prosperity. The Fund is required to exercise surveillance over their exchange rate policies and over the international monetary system. It maintains a large pool of currencies from which to help finance the temporary imbalances of its members, and this financial assistance – provided for short-term to medium-term periods and usually subject to conditions – allows member countries to correct their payment imbalances without having to resort to the trade and payment restrictions that they have pledged themselves to avoid. The policy adjustment that countries make in connection with the use of Fund resources support their creditworthiness and thereby facilitate their access to financial markets. In 1969, the Fund created SDRs (special drawing rights) as a reserve asset.

The work of the Fund is carried out by a Board of Governors, an Executive Board, a Managing Director, and staff. Each member country is represented by a Governor and an Alternate Governor on the Board of Governors, which is the Fund's senior decision-making body. The Board of Governors meets annually, but may be asked by the Executive Board to vote on important matters by mail or cable between meetings. A member country's voting power is related to its subscription to the Fund's financial resources, and is broadly reflective of its relative size in the world economy (i.e. trade, gross national product and monetary reserves). The daily business of the Fund is conducted at its headquarters in Washington, DC, by an Executive Board consisting of twenty-two Executive Directors, chaired by the Managing Director. Each of the five members having the largest quotas, and thus the highest voting power – the United States, the United Kingdom, Germany, France and Japan – appoints an Executive Director. In addition, if the Fund's two largest creditor members are not among these five, they may each appoint an Executive Director. Currently, Saudi Arabia appoints an Executive Director on this basis. Sixteen Executive Directors are elected by members or groups of member countries.

The Board of Governors is advised on policy issues by two ministerial-level committees whose membership reflects that of the Executive Board: the Interim Committee of the Board of Governors on the International Monetary System and the Joint Ministerial

Committee of the World Bank and the Fund on the Transfer of Real Resources to Developing Countries (the Development Committee). The Interim and Developing Committees normally meet twice a year – in the spring at Fund headquarters in Washington, and in the autumn at the site of the Annual Meetings of the Fund and Bank, just prior to those meetings.

The Fund also maintains small permanent offices in Paris, in Geneva, and at the United Nations in New York.

### Exchange-rate policies

Since the early 1970s, the international monetary system has undergone major changes. The Bretton Woods agreement, founded on a system of par values fixed in terms of gold, came to an end in practice after the decision by the United States in 1971 no longer to convert dollars into gold or other reserve assets. As a consequence, countries are free to choose their exchange arrangements, a situation recognised in the Second Amendment (1978) to the Fund's Articles of Agreement. The major economic countries have opted for a freely floating exchange rate, but the majority of individual countries maintain a fixed exchange rate pegged either to another currency, to the SDR – which is valued in terms of a basket of five currencies – or to some other basket of major currencies. The members of the European Monetary System (EMS) undertake to maintain fixed margins for the exchange rates of their currencies *vis-à-vis* other currencies within the group, but the rates for these currencies are allowed to fluctuate with respect to currencies outside the group. Realignments in the EMS take place after consultation within the group.

### Consultation

The Fund conducts consultations with each member country – in principle, annually – to appraise the member's economic and financial situation and policies. The consultation procedure begins with meetings in the member country between Fund staff and representatives of the member government. On the basis of these discussions, the staff prepares a report on economic conditions and policies for the Executive Board. The Board then discusses and comments on the report. The Board's views, as summarised by the Managing Director, are then transmitted to the member government by the Fund.

### Quotas and resources

The Fund's resources stem largely from its members' subscriptions, and these are based on a quota system which broadly reflects a member's weight in the world economy. Quotas also determine the voting power of members, their contributions to the Fund's resources, their access to these resources, and their share in allocations of SDRs.

While subscriptions constitute its basic resources, the Fund supplements them by borrowing. Under the General Arrangements to Borrow (GAB), which became effective in October 1962, ten industrial member countries together with non-member Switzerland (constituting the eleven-nation 'Group of Ten') extended credit lines to the Fund. The GAB has been renewed periodically, and in 1984 Saudi Arabia associated itself with the other eleven participants.

*Financial facilities*

Members have access to the financial resources of the Fund under a variety of permanent and temporary facilities to help meet balance of payments needs. The mechanics of the transaction are as follows. The member uses its own currency to 'purchase' from the Fund an equivalent amount of the currencies of other members (or SDRs), and these in turn can be used to finance the member's balance of payments deficit or to supply its need for reserves. Within a specific period – or earlier if the member's balance of payments and reserve position improves – the member must repay the Fund by repurchasing with SDRs or the currencies of other members specified by the Fund the amount of its own currency that it used in order to make the drawing, except to the extent that the Fund sells the member's currency. Credit from the Fund is available in four tranches, each tranche being the equivalent of 25 per cent of the quota.

If the country suffers serious payments imbalances related to structural problems in production, trade, or prices, the adjustment process is likely to require both a longer period of time and greater resources than normally permitted under the credit tranche facility. In such situations, the member may make use of the *Extended Fund Facility*, under which up to 140 per cent of its quota may be purchased beyond the first credit tranche. Depending on whether the credit tranche or the extended Fund facility is used, resources are provided through lines of credit called stand-by or extended arrangements, and normally take place over a period of one year, although the period may be extended up to three years. Drawings are repayable within three to five years under the credit tranche facility and four to ten years under the extended Fund facility.

When a member receives financial assistance under the Fund's credit facilities, it must adopt a programme of specific measures to overcome its payments imbalance and thus provide assurance that it can repay the funds received. This aspect of Fund policies is known as *conditionality*. The Fund staff help member countries design adjustment programmes having due regard to their domestic, social and political objectives, economic priorities, and general circumstances. Drawings under both the credit tranche policy and the extended Fund facility are subject to a one-time service charge of 0.5 per cent, plus a charge at an annual rate on outstanding drawings.

The Fund also makes resources available under two special purpose facilities: the compensatory and the buffer stock financing facilities. *Compensatory financing* is available to members facing payments difficulties resulting from temporary shortfalls in their export earnings that are due largely to conditions beyond their control, such as falling commodity prices or natural disasters, including bad weather. In 1981, this facility was broadened to provide assistance to members facing payments difficulties owing to an excess in the cost of cereal imports. *Buffer stock financing*, available up to 45 per cent of quota, is available to members having payments difficulties to finance their contributions to international buffer stocks that are maintained to stabilise world markets for commodities.

*Structural adjustment facility*
The Structural Adjustment Facility provides loans to low-income member countries that are facing protracted balance of payments problems and that agree to undertake medium-term structural adjustment programmes.

*SDRs (Special Drawing Rights)*
The SDR is an international reserve asset created by the Fund to supplement existing reserve assets. It is the unit of account of the Fund, and is also used as such by a number of international and regional organisations and in capital markets as a denominator and a unit of contract, such as in SDR-denominated deposits with commercial banks. It is the members' declared intention, expressed in the Fund's Articles, that the SDR shall eventually become the principal reserve asset in the international monetary system. The method of valuation of the SDR is determined by the Fund, and since January 1981, the 'basket' has consisted of the currencies of the five members with the highest value of exports of goods and services.

*Technical assistance*
Member countries of the Fund may make use of its technical assistance for helping to improve the management of their economies. Experts sent to member countries by the Fund advise on fiscal, monetary, and balance of payments policies, central and

general banking, statistics, accounting, exchange and trade systems, and operational aspects of Fund policies.

## INTERNATIONAL CIVIL AVIATION ORGANISATION

Established in 1944 in Chicago, ICAO was formed to assure the safe, orderly and economic development of world civil air transportation. ICAO has developed a worldwide system of standards, practices and rules common to all nations. The Organisation serves the world today as a medium through which 164 nations cooperate to ensure safety for the air-travelling public and for agreement in the technical, economic and legal fields of civil aviation.

The legislative body of ICAO is the Assembly which is composed of representatives of all member states and meets at least once in three years to review in detail the work of the Organisation performed during the last triennium and to decide on future policies.

The Council, which is the executive body of ICAO, comprises thirty-three members elected by the Assembly; they must be representative of the major civil aviation interests and facilities, as well as providing representation on a worldwide basis. The Council is responsible to the Assembly and meets in virtually continuous session. One of the major duties of the Council is to adopt international standards and recommended practices and to incorporate these as Annexes to the Convention on International Civil Aviation. It directs the work of the Organisation, establishes and supervises subsidiary technical committees, can act as arbiter between member states on matters concerning the interpretation and application of the Chicago Convention, provides technical assistance to developing nations, elects the President, appoints the Secretary-General, administers the finances of the Organisation and considers any matter relating to the Convention which any contracting state refers to it.

The Council is assisted by the Air Navigation Commission (in technical matters), the Air Transport Committee (in economic matters), the Committee on Joint Support of Air Navigation Services, the Finance Committee and the Legal Committee.

The headquarters of ICAO are in Montreal and there are regional offices in Bangkok, Cairo, Dakar, Lima, Mexico City, Nairobi and Paris.

## UNIVERSAL POSTAL UNION

The UPU is responsible for the maintenance and development of postal services throughout the world. It has its headquarters in Berne and is controlled by the Universal Postal Congress composed of all member states meeting every five years and a permanent Executive Council of forty elected on a geographical basis by the Congress which meets annually.

## INTERNATIONAL TELECOMMUNICATIONS UNION

The ITU is the body responsible for international cooperation, research and the dissemination of knowledge in all branches of telecommunications, and for the administration of its Convention. Policy decisions are made by a Plenipotentiary Conference of all member states meeting every five years; executive control lies with the Administrative Council elected by the Assembly and meeting annually, and their four permanent organs: the General Secretariat (situated in Geneva), the International Frequency Registration Board, the International Radio Consultative Committee and the International Telegraph and Telephone Consultative Committee.

## WORLD METEOROLOGICAL ORGANISATION

The WMO seeks to maintain and improve international cooperation and coordination in the field of meteorological services, in particular the exchange and standardisation of weather data and the establishment of a worldwide network of meteorological stations. It encourages research and training in meteorology, and furthers the study of the application of meteorology to shipping, water usage, agriculture, and other human activities. It has its headquarters and Secretariat in Geneva and is controlled by the World Meteorological Congress composed of the heads of the meteorological services of member states meeting every four years and an Executive Committee of twenty-nine meeting annually.

## INTERNATIONAL MARITIME ORGANISATION

The organisation changed its name from Inter-governmental Maritime Consultative Organisation (IMCO) to International Maritime Organisation (IMO) in May 1982. It is responsible for international cooperation in all technical matters relating to shipping. It was established on the basis of the Maritime Convention which resulted from the United Nations Maritime Conference held in Geneva in 1948, and seeks to improve maritime safety and prevent maritime pollution from ships, disseminates information, convenes conferences, and promotes and administers international maritime conventions. It has its headquarters and Secretariat in London and is controlled by an Assembly of all member states meeting every second year and a Council of twenty-four. There are four main Committees: on maritime safety, legal matters, marine environment protection, and technical cooperation.

## WORLD INTELLECTUAL PROPERTY ORGANISATION

WIPO became a Specialised Agency in December 1974, and is responsible for the promotion, through cooperation among member states, of worldwide protection of Intellectual Property which the Organisation defines as inventions, trademarks, designs and copyrights. The agency is also responsible for the administration of various 'Unions' comprising groups of states which are parties to a particular Convention, e.g. the Berne Convention on Copyright. A substantial part of the activities and resources of WIPO is devoted to assistance in developing countries, particular emphasis being laid on the transfer of technology. The headquarters of the organisation are in Geneva, where an annual Conference of all member states is held to plan the next year's activities and budget, and also where the majority of the almost daily technical meetings are held. The conference is normally a joint one with the General Assembly of those states party to the Berne or Paris 'Unions'.

## INTERNATIONAL FUND FOR AGRICULTURAL DEVELOPMENT

The agreement establishing the International Fund for Agricultural Development (IFAD) was adopted on 13 June 1976 at a United Nations conference. It was opened for signature on 20 December 1976, following the attainment of initial pledges of $1 billion, and entered into force on 30 November 1977. The main purpose of IFAD is to mobilise additional resources to help developing countries improve their food production and nutrition, fisheries, processing and storage – and concentrates on rural areas. Its primary goal is to help efforts to end chronic hunger and malnutrition. It lends money for projects which will have a significant impact on improving food production in developing countries, particularly for the benefit of the poorest sections of the rural populations. It seeks to bring small farmers and the landless into the development process: thus, the fund is concerned not only with production objectives but with the impact each project may have on employment, nutrition and income distribution. Loan operations of IFAD fall into two groups: projects initiated by the Fund and projects 'co-financed' with other financial and development institutions, such as the World Bank and IDA and the various development banks (African, Asian, Inter-American, Islamic). IFAD loans represent only a part of total project costs; the governments concerned contribute a share.

The Fund's operations are directed by the Governing Council, on which all member states are represented, each of the three categories of members (developed countries, oil-exporting developing countries and other developing countries) having the same number of votes. Thus, the donor countries hold two-thirds of the total number of votes and the developing countries, at the same time, hold two-thirds of the votes. Current operations are overseen by the Executive Board, composed of eighteen Executive Directors, six from each of the three constituent categories, and eighteen alternates, and chaired by the President of the Fund. The headquarters of the fund are in Rome.

## GENERAL AGREEMENTS ON TARIFFS AND TRADE

GATT as an organisation derives from a multilateral treaty signed in 1947 by twenty-three major trading nations for the limitation and reduction of trade barriers and the establishment of rules for international trade.

A basic principle (article I of the General Agreement) is that trade must be conducted on a non-discriminatory basis: all signatories must give one another treatment as favourable as they give to any country in the application and administration of import and export duties and charges. As an exception, article XXIV permits regional trading arrangements (such as the EC, and Free Trade Areas) providing for the elimination of duties and other barriers to substantially all trade between countries in the group. A further important exception, authorised initially by temporary waiver but now established as a permanent rule, permits tariff preferences granted by developed in favour of developing countries (the *Generalised System of Preferences* negotiated by UNCTAD) and by developing countries to one another. Other special provisions recognising the particular trade problems of developing countries are found in various articles, and especially part IV of the Agreement.

GATT provides the contracting parties with a forum for discussing trade problems, for reconciling disputes concerning the interpretation of the treaty, and for the grant of waivers (exemptions from the rules in special instances). In addition GATT has organised negotiating conferences or 'rounds', e.g. the Kennedy and Tokyo Rounds, and the latest (eighth) round, the Uruguay Round, launched in Punta del Este, Uruguay in 1986, designed to produce substantial reductions in tariff and non-tariff barriers to trade, and in revision of the trade rules in response to changing circumstances. A further initiative is the International Trade Centre operated in conjunction with UNCTAD which provides valuable services and advice in marketing and trade problems. The Director-General and Secretariat of GATT are in Geneva, and it is controlled by an annual Session of Contracting Parties and a Council of Representatives which meets in the intervening period approximately once a month.

There are 103 signatories to GATT, together accounting for over four-fifths of world trade, and thirty-nine other countries accept its conditions.

## UNITED NATIONS DEVELOPMENT PROGRAMME

UNDP became a specialised agency of the UN on January 1 1986. It is an amalgam of the United Nations Special Fund and the Expanded Technical Assistance Programme providing technical advice and aid to developing countries, its funds being obtained from donations by member states. In partnership with governments it undertakes high priority, pre-investment projects; makes available experts and consultants as well as specialised equipment and contract services, and offers fellowship awards for training abroad. Assistance is given in support of projects to increase agricultural and industrial productivity, to conduct feasibility studies and to establish or expand applied research institutes and facilities for training and education, as well as to strengthen the administrative and institutional framework for development, and work in a variety of other essential fields.

The UNDP is controlled by a Governing Council composed of forty-eight members elected by ECOSOC and maintains Resident Representatives in nearly one hundred recipient countries. Its headquarters are in New York.

# SUBSIDIARY ORGANISATIONS

As the United Nations has developed, the General Assembly has found it necessary to establish several new organisations in order to fulfil its obligations satisfactorily. All vary considerably in scope and constitution, but all depend ultimately on the General Assembly.

## UNITED NATIONS CONFERENCE ON TRADE AND DEVELOPMENT

UNCTAD originally met in 1964 as a Conference convened by the General Assembly in order to help restructure the traditional patterns of international trade in the interests of developing countries. It became institutionalised as an organ of the General Assembly, and reports to the General Assembly through the Economic and Social Council. Its purpose is to obtain fair and stable prices for primary commodities, to facilitate trade and development, and in particular to enable developing countries to gain access to the markets of developed countries. It has its headquarters and secretariat in Geneva, and is controlled by a Conference of its members meeting every four years and a Trade and Development Board consisting of 124 members elected by the Conference and meeting annually. It has seven main Committees: Shipping; Manufactures; Commodities: Invisibles and Financing related to Trade; Economic Cooperation among Developing Countries, Transfer of Technology and the special Committee on Preferences; also various sub-committees, working parties and *ad hoc* committees of experts. Among the major achievements of UNCTAD are the Generalised System of Preferences and the concept of solidarity and cooperation among developing countries.

## UNITED NATIONS HIGH COMMISSION FOR REFUGEES

UNHCR endeavours to assist and find permanent settlement for refugees. It is an integral part of the UN Secretariat and receives grants from the UN Budget for limited periods, which are periodically renewed. Specific programmes and the provision of emergency relief are financed from voluntary contributions. It has its headquarters in Geneva and is controlled and directed by a Committee reporting to ECOSOC and the General Assembly. The High Commissioner is elected by the General Assembly on the recommendation of the Secretary-General of the United Nations.

## UNITED NATIONS CHILDREN'S EMERGENCY FUND

UNICEF provides aid and welfare to children throughout the world. It assists specific projects in the fields of health, nutrition, family and child welfare, education and vocational training; provides basic equipment for maternal and child health centres, and training and stipends for their staff; helps campaigns against endemic diseases;

encourages increased production and consumption of protective foods; provides aid for basic social services for children in developing countries, and emergency help to children who are victims of floods, earthquake, drought or other disasters. It comes under the aegis of ECOSOC and obtains its funds in the form of donations from governments and private sources. It has its headquarters in the United Nations Secretariat in New York and is under the control of an Executive Board of thirty meeting once a year. The Executive Director is appointed by the UN Secretary-General in consultation with the Board.

## UNITED NATIONS INSTITUTE FOR TRAINING AND RESEARCH

UNITAR seeks to contribute to the process of modernisation and development through the better use of the training of human resources. It carries out training programmes in diplomatic practice, international organisation and technical and economic cooperation, and has as a major objective the creation of a corps of personnel of the highest calibre, particularly from the developing countries, equipped to serve in assignments within the United Nations or with national services connected with the work of the UN. A Board of Trustees determines policy, and the Executive Director and headquarters are in New York.

## UNITED NATIONS RELIEF AND WORKS AGENCY FOR PALESTINE REFUGEES IN THE NEAR EAST

UNRWA provides aid and assistance to Palestine refugees in the Near East, and endeavours to arrange for their permanent settlement; it was originally established as an *ad hoc* committee by the United Nations General Assembly, and is supported by donations from governments and private sources. Its main concern is the provision of food, clothing and shelter, education and health services. It is controlled by an Advisory Committee, and the Commissioner-General has his headquarters in Beirut.

## UNITED NATIONS INDUSTRIAL DEVELOPMENT ORGANISATION

UNIDO was established by the General Assembly in 1966 for the purpose of encouraging and implementing United Nations efforts in the field of industrial development, particularly by carrying out research studies on behalf of developing countries. Its governing body, the Industrial Development Board, is elected by the General Assembly and reports to the Assembly through ECOSOC; and its Secretariat is at the UN City in Vienna.

## THE WORLD FOOD PROGRAMME

The World Food Programme was established jointly by the United Nations and the Food and Agriculture Organisation as a result of the resolution of the World Food Conference. Its purpose is to assist and provide a focus for multilateral food aid. It is administered by a joint UN/FAO Committee and staff, and its Executive Director is appointed jointly by the Secretary-General of the UN and the Director-General of the FAO.

## UNITED NATIONS ENVIRONMENT PROGRAMME

The UNEP was established as a result of the United Nations Conference on the Human Environment held in Stockholm in 1973. Its major purpose is to encourage and coordinate policies for the reduction of pollution in its various forms, and to carry out research and relevant studies. Its headquarters and Secretariat are in Nairobi.

## UNITED NATIONS FUND FOR POPULATION ACTIVITIES

The UNFPA was established in 1967 and comes under the direction of the Administrator of the UNDP. The Fund considers the wider aspects of population activities including the status of women and the need to overcome minority regimes. It concentrates on monitoring population trends and evaluating national policies, and reports at intervals to the Economic and Social Council on its findings. A major objective was the holding of a population census by member countries between 1975 and 1985.

## THE INTERNATIONAL LAW COMMISSION

The ILC was set up by resolution of the UN General Assembly in November 1947. The body consists of thirty-four distinguished international lawyers, who are elected by the General Assembly for a five-year period of office, and exists to encourage 'the progressive development of international law and its codification'. The members of the Commission are not government representatives but are elected on a personal basis and sit in their personal capacity as experts. The geographical representation is as follows: Africa 8, Asia 7, Latin America 6, Eastern Europe 3, Africa or Eastern Europe (in rotation) 1, Asia or Latin America (in rotation) 1; other areas 8. The ILC conducts its sessions in Geneva.

THE UN CONFERENCE ON DISARMAMENT AND THE DISARMAMENT COMMISSION

The Conference on Disarmament stems from an agreement by the USA, USSR, France and UK in 1959 to set up a Ten Nation Committee on Disarmament to include representatives of their four countries together with Bulgaria, Canada, Czechoslovakia, Italy, Poland and Romania. In 1961 it was expanded into an Eighteen Nation Disarmament Committee, and again in 1969 to twenty-six members, when it was renamed the Conference of the Committee on Disarmament (CCD). At the first UN Special Session on Disarmament in 1978 it was increased to forty members, and its name was changed back to the Committee on Disarmament (CD). Its name was changed again to the Conference on Disarmament in 1984. The Conference meets twice a year, from February to April and from June to August, in Geneva. It is the only multilateral negotiating body of the international community as a whole in the field of disarmament.

The UN Disarmament Commission (UNDC), in contrast, is a deliberative body. It was first formed under the Security Council in 1952 with a membership of eleven states, subsequently increased to twenty-five in 1957 and then a year later it was increased to comprise all members of the UN. The UNDC did not meet from 1965 until 1979, following its revival by the first Special Session on Disarmament. Substantive sessions of the UNDC are held once a year in New York.

HUMAN RIGHTS

International intervention in support of human rights has existed for a very long time and in a wide variety of forms. It received a major impetus with the adoption of the Covenant of the League of Nations and the subsequent establishment of the International Labour Organisation in 1919, but human rights in the widest sense became a definitive factor in international relations with the adoption of the *Universal Declaration of Human Rights* by the General Assembly on 10 December 1948. The Assembly called upon all member countries to publicise the text and 'to cause it to be disseminated, displayed, read and expounded principally in schools and other educational institutions, without distinction based on the political status of countries or territories'.

On the basis of the Declaration, two international covenants have been drawn up:

- the *International Convention on Economic, Social and Cultural Rights* which came into effect on 3 January 1976 and which has been ratified or acceded to by eight-four states; and
- the *International Covenant on Civil and Political Rights* and the *Optional Protocol* which came into force on 23 March 1976. Eighty-one states have ratified or acceded to the Covenant, and thirty-four have ratified or acceded to the Optional Protocol.

It is the responsibility of the Economic and Social Council, in terms of article 62 of the Charter, to 'make recommendations for the purpose of promoting respect for, and observance of, human rights and fundamental freedoms for all', and such matters are normally dealt with by the Council's Second (Social) Committee. The Council has also established the *Commission on Human Rights* and the *Commission on the Status of Women*.

*The Commission on Human Rights* meets annually for a period of approximately six weeks and may concern itself with any matter relating to human rights. It is composed of representatives of forty-three member states, and its subsidiary bodies include the Sub-Commission on the Prevention of Discrimination and Protection of Minorities, and various working parties.

*The Commission on the Status of Women* is composed of representatives of thirty-two member states of the United Nations and meets twice a year for periods of three weeks. Its main task is to prepare draft resolutions and decisions for consideration by the Economic and Social Council, and on 18 December 1979 the General Assembly adopted the *Convention on the Elimination of All Forms of Discrimination against Women* which entered into force on 3 September 1981. This establishes, *inter alia*, a twenty-three-member Committee on the Elimination of Discrimination against Women which reports annually to the General Assembly.

*The Human Rights Committee* was established in 1977 under the provisions of the International Covenant on Civil and Political

Rights in order to monitor the progress of member states in the implementation of human rights. It consists of eighteen members of high moral character and recognised competence in the field of human rights, elected by states which are party to the Convention from among their nationals and who act in a personal capacity for a four-year term. The Committee may receive complaints from states and also, in respect of those states signatories of the Optional Protocol, from individuals. It normally holds three sessions annually, and reports to the General Assembly.

The task of enforcing human rights is constantly to the forefront of United Nations activities, and in addition to the formal framework established under the Charter, the General Assembly and its specialised agencies have from time to time agreed Declarations and resolutions on pressing issues such as Apartheid and all forms of racial discrimination, the rights of Palestinians, Victims of Torture and Migrant Workers, as well as on situations arising in specific countries.

## THE INTERNATIONAL RESEARCH AND TRAINING INSTITUTE FOR THE ADVANCEMENT OF WOMEN

INSTRAW was established by the General Assembly in 1985 and seeks to stimulate and assist, through research, training and the collection and exchange of information, the efforts of intergovernmental, governmental and non-governmental organisations aimed at the advancement of women in development both as participants and beneficiaries. The Institute is funded by voluntary contributions and is situated in Santo Domingo, Dominican Republic.

## OTHER CONSULTATIVE BODIES

Of the special committees and commissions set up by the General Assembly from time to time for specific purposes those listed above have acquired a permanent or semi-permanent nature; others, equally dependent on the General Assembly, have not become institutionalised to the same extent. In addition to those with a purely organisational or administrative function they deal with peace-keeping and security, political matters, decolonisation and questions relating to trusteeship, legal, scientific, and educational matters; they include

Commission for the Unification and Rehabilitation of Korea
Committee on the Peaceful Uses of Outer Space
Conciliation Commission for Palestine

Scientific Committee on the Effects of Radiation
Special Committee on the Implementation of the Declaration on the Granting of Independence to Colonial Countries and Peoples ('The Special Committee of twenty-four')
Special Committee on Apartheid
Working Group on Direct Broadcasting Satellites
United Nations University (Tokyo)
World Food Council
Special Committee on Peace-Keeping Operations.

*Chapter 8*

# INTERNATIONAL ORGANISATIONS AND AGREEMENTS OUTSIDE THE UNITED NATIONS

## THE LEAGUE OF ARAB STATES

The League of Arab States is an association of states having a common heritage and mutual interests, based on the Cairo Pact of the League of Arab States in 1945, supplemented by the 1959 Treaty of Mutual Defence and Cooperation. The objects of the League are to strengthen the bonds between member states; to coordinate their political activities so as to ensure their independence and sovereignty, and to promote the interests of Arab countries. It also seeks close collaboration in the fields of culture, health, social welfare, transport and communications, passports, visas and nationality laws, and economic and financial matters including trade, customs, currency, agriculture and industry; and provides that in the event of aggression or a threat of aggression a member state may request a meeting of the Council of the League. The member states are Algeria, Bahrain, Jibuti, Egypt, Iraq, Jordan, Kuwait, Lebanon, Libya, Mauritania, Morocco, Oman, Palestine, Qatar, Saudi Arabia, Somalia, Sudan, Syria, Tunisia, United Arab Emirates, and Yemen. The League of Arab States has observer status in the General Assembly and in its subsidiary organisations; and the Secretariat and Headquarters of the League are in Cairo.

## ASSOCIATION OF SOUTH-EAST ASIAN NATIONS

ASEAN is based on the Declaration signed in Bangkok on 8 August 1967, the aim of the Organisation being to accelerate the socio-economic and cultural development of all member states through peaceful and harmonious relations. Cooperation extends over a wide range of subjects including agriculture and forestry, trade and industry, transport and communications, finance and banking, social welfare, labour, health, natural disasters, narcotics, law, education, youth, science and technology and the environment. Although the emphasis in the Declaration was on non-political forms of co-operation, ASEAN signed a Declaration on the Zone of Peace Freedom and Neutrality (ZOPFAN), in 1971, in order to keep the region free from superpower rivalry. In February 1976, a Treaty of Amity and Cooperation in Southeast Asia and the Declaration of ASEAN Accord were signed. Both are designed to promote friendly and harmonious relations amongst Southeast Asian countries, the former outlining the methods for the peaceful settlement of disputes.

At the apex of the ASEAN structure is the Summit of the Heads of State and Government, who meet every three years. ASEAN Ministerial Meetings at the Foreign Ministers' level are held annually to coordinate all ASEAN activities; Economic Ministers' Meetings have been held regularly since 1975, while the Ministers of Agriculture, Energy, Information, Tourism, Labour, Social Welfare and Environment have held meetings from time to time.

The Singapore Summit agreed to the establishment of the ASEAN Free Trade Area (AFTA), as from 1 January 1993, using the Common Effective Preferential Tariff (CEPT) scheme as the main mechanism, with the ultimate effective tariffs ranging from 0–5%. The CEPT scheme will cover manufactured products, including capital goods and processed agricultural products, but agricultural products are to be excluded from the CEPT scheme. In addition, ASEAN has evolved a system of consultations with its main trading partners through the 'dialogue process'. The Dialogue Partners are Australia, Canada, Japan, South Korea, New Zealand, the United States of America, the European Commission, and the United Nations Development Programme. With the exception of the UNDP, ASEAN Foreign Ministers meet their counterparts from these countries annually. The Secretariat, headed by the Secretary General of ASEAN, is in Jakarta.

# BANK FOR INTERNATIONAL SETTLEMENTS

The BIS was founded as a result of an intergovernmental Convention dated 20 January 1930. It is an international bank which makes its services available to central banks and intergovernmental institutions. It is also a centre for economic and monetary research and consultations, and acts as technical agent and for the execution of certain specific agreements with, for example, the OECD and the ECSC. It cooperates with other institutions such as the IMF, and since 1982 has been particularly instrumental in resolving liquidity problems of debtor countries by providing short-term bridging loans. Its membership comprises nearly all European central banks, as well as the monetary authorities of a number of non-European countries: thirty-one including Japan and the USA; and although some of the shares are held by the public, all rights of voting and representation in respect of the shares are vested in the central bank of each country in which the shares were issued. Under its statutes the BIS may only undertake operations that are in conformity with the monetary policy of the central banks concerned, and its operations are essentially short term. The headquarters of the Bank are in Basel.

# BLACK SEA ECONOMIC COOPERATION

The Black Sea Pact is a tentative regional organisation of eleven states established to coordinate activities in the fields of transport, communications, ecology, investment, power, and related economic matters. Its members are Albania, Armenia, Azerbaijan, Bulgaria, Georgia, Greece, Moldava, Romania, Russia, Turkey and Ukraine.

# CARIBBEAN REGIONAL ORGANISATIONS

*The Caribbean Community* (CARICOM) is the major regional organisation in the Caribbean. Its main function is the creation of a Caribbean Common Market but its activities extend to a wider sphere and include the harmonisation of economic and related policies. Members are Antigua and Bahamas, Barbuda, Barbados, Belize, Dominica, Grenada, Guyana, Jamaica, Montserrat, St Christopher-Nevis, St Lucia, St Vincent and the Grenadines, Trinidad and Tobago, Turks and Caicos Islands, and the British Virgin Islands.

The Heads of Government Conference is responsible for the policy of the Community, and the Common Market Council of Ministers is responsible for the Common Market. The Secretariat is in Georgetown, Guyana.

*The Organisation of Eastern Caribbean States* (OECS) consists of Antigua and Barbuda, Dominica, Grenada, Montserrat, St Christopher-Nevis, St Lucia and St Vincent and the Grenadines, all of which have in the past shared certain common services such as a common currency and judiciary. These common services are being extended to include, *inter alia*, harmonisation of foreign policies and joint overseas diplomatic representation.

# CENTRAL AMERICAN COMMON MARKET

The members of MCCA (which has been recently re-established) are Costa Rica, El Salvador, Guatemala, Honduras and Nicaragua. In terms of the 1960 treaty of Managua the parties aim to eliminate tariffs on nearly all intra-regional trade, and eventually to create a customs union. They envisage the harmonisation of policies relating to taxation, customs, classification, monopolies, dumping and unfair trade practices; the acceptance of the principles of coordinated industrial development and of freedom of transit, and the establishment of a Central American Bank of Economic Integration. The institutions of MCCA are the Central American Economic Council composed of Ministers of each of the parties, and an Executive Council on which each party is represented. The Secretary-General and the Secretariat are in Guatemala City.

# CENTRAL EUROPEAN INITIATIVE

Originally the Pentagonale and subsequently the Hexagonale, the Central European Initiative is a tentative regional organisation established in order to foster close cooperation in an area of traditional mutual interest. Members are Austria, Croatia, Czech Republic, Hungary, Italy, Poland, Slovenia and Slovakia.

# THE COMMONWEALTH

The Commonwealth is an association of states and dependent territories all of which at one time formed part of the British Empire or were Protected States in treaty relations with the Crown. Intra-Commonwealth cooperation and consultation are maintained by institutional and personal contact in cultural and educational matters; and meetings of heads of governments or their representatives are held normally every two years for the exchange of views on matters of common concern. Aid and development are featured in the initiation of the Colombo Plan and in the Commonwealth Fellowships; and trade, in preferential tariff and quota arrangements, now mainly incorporated in the Lomé Convention. Her Majesty Queen Elizabeth II is Head of the Commonwealth, and the Commonwealth Secretariat and its Secretary-General are situated in London. The following states are full members of the Commonwealth: Antigua and Barbuda, Australia, Bahamas, Bangladesh, Barbados, Belize, Botswana, Brunei, Canada, Cyprus, Dominica, Fiji, The Gambia, Ghana, Grenada, Guyana, India, Jamaica, Kenya, Kiribati, Lesotho, Malawi, Pakistan, Malaysia, Maldives, Malta, Mauritius, Namibia, Nauru, New Zealand, Nigeria, Papua New Guinea, St Christopher and Nevis, St Lucia, St Vincent and the Grenadines, Seychelles, Sierra Leone, Singapore, Solomon Islands, Sri Lanka, Swaziland, Tanzania, Tonga, Trinidad and Tobago, Tuvalu, Uganda, the United Kingdom of Great Britain and Northern Ireland, Vanuatu, Western Samoa, Zambia and Zimbabwe. The Commonwealth Parliamentary Association provides a focus for the mutual interests of the legislatures of the Commonwealth; those member states which fail to maintain the concept or practice of parliamentary government being suspended from membership of the Association.

# THE COMMONWEALTH OF INDEPENDENT STATES

The Commonwealth of Independent States was formed at the end of 1991 by eleven of the fifteen Republics of the former Soviet Union. It is an informal confederation of independent states which seeks to harmonise the transition from a command economy to a market-driven economy, and if they see fit, from a joint military command to independent political control of the armed forces. In this connection its major task, as far as the interests of the rest of the world are concerned, is to establish effective control over the former Soviet nuclear know-how and capability. The Commonwealth will also have the task of resolving inherited ethnic inconsistencies, of ensuring the fair distribution of food and fuel, of coordinating currencies and transport, and of providing a forum for the resolution of the daunting and multifarious problems stemming from the dissolution of the most powerful and centralised empire in Europe's history.

The member states of the Commonwealth are Armenia, Azerbaijan, Belarus, Kazakhstan, Kyrgyzstan, Moldova, Russia, Tajikistan, Turkmenistan, Ukraine and Uzbekistan; and the secretariat of the Commonwealth is in Minsk.

# CONFERENCE ON SECURITY AND COOPERATION IN EUROPE

The CSCE, having been established during the Cold War with relatively little credibility, has now become the only organisation with the potential for promoting security and cooperation in Europe, and between the two major nuclear member states, the United States and Russia. Whether or not that potential will be realised will depend on the political will of the governments concerned. Under pressure of recent events, the emphasis within the CSCE has shifted from regional security to the peaceful settlement of ethnic disputes in the newly democratic states of Europe, exemplified by the appointment of a High Commission for Minorities. A Conflict Prevention Centre has been established in Vienna and an Office for Democratic Institutions and Human Rights (ODIHR) in Warsaw; the secretariat of the organisation is in Prague. Meetings at Ministerial level take place once a year in the capital of one of the participating States. All decisions are taken by consensus. The Minister for Foreign Affairs of the host country of such a Ministerial Meeting (Council) acts as Chairman in Office of the CSCE until the next Council meeting.

Participating States are: Albania, Armenia, Austria, Azerbaijan, Belarus, Belgium, Bosnia and Herzegovina, Bulgaria, Canada, Cyprus, Croatia, the Czech Republic, Denmark, Estonia, Finland, France, Georgia, Germany, Greece, Holy See, Hungary, Ireland, Iceland, Italy, Kazakhstan, Kyrgyzstan, Latvia, Liechtenstein, Lithuania, Luxembourg, Malta, Moldova, Monaco, Norway, the Netherlands, Poland, Portugal, Romania, Russia, San Marino, the Slovak Republic, Slovenia, Spain, Sweden, Switzerland, Tajikistan, Turkmenistan, Turkey, Ukraine, United Kingdom, Uzbekistan and United States of America.

# COUNCIL OF EUROPE

The Council of Europe was the first international organisation established in Europe after the 1939–45 war, and in terms of its Statute signed on 5 May 1949 by the ten founder countries its objective is to work for greater European unity, to uphold the principles of parliamentary democracy, to promote human values, and improve living conditions. Currently its major concerns are human rights; education, culture and sport, social questions, youth unemployment, public health; environment and architectural heritage; local and regional authorities and legal affairs. Major achievements of the Council have been the European Convention on Human Rights, and the establishment of the European Commission and Court of Human Rights, whose jurisdiction has now been accepted as compulsory by nineteen member states, and the European Convention on the Suppression of Terrorism, which, *inter alia* defines offences that shall *not* be regarded as political offences or as offences connected with a political offence or as offences inspired by political motives. Membership consists of Austria, Belgium, Bulgaria, Cyprus, the Czech Republic, Denmark, Estonia, Finland, France, Germany, Greece, Hungary, Iceland, Ireland, Italy, Liechtenstein, Lithuania, Luxembourg, Malta, the Netherlands, Norway, Portugal, Poland, San Marino, the Slovak Republic, Slovenia, Spain, Sweden, Switzerland, Turkey and the United Kingdom. The institutions of the Council are the Committee of Ministers of all member states which meets twice a year; the meetings of Permanent Representatives (Deputies) which last for approximately one week each month, and the Parliamentary Assembly of 210 members, which is a consultative body and which meets three times a year. The Secretariat-General is in Strasbourg.

## ECONOMIC COOPERATION ORGANISATION

A Regional group for economic cooperation, consisting of Azerbaijan, Iran, Pakistan, Turkey, Turkmenistan and Uzbekistan; with Kazakhstan, Kyrgyzstan and Tajikistan as observers.

## THE EUROPEAN COMMUNITY

The EC consists of twelve member states: Belgium, Denmark, France, Germany, Greece, Ireland, Italy, Luxembourg, the Netherlands, Portugal, Spain and the United Kingdom. They are signatories of, or have subsequently acceded to, the 1957 Treaty of Rome, the 1986 Single European Act, the 1992 Maastricht Treaty on European Union and the various Treaties of Accession; and Association Agreements offering limited facilities have been entered into with various countries in the region. The member states of the EC have, together with the member states of the European Free Trade Association (except for Switzerland, but including Liechtenstein), created a Free Trade Area with free movement of manufactured goods, capital, services and persons of the eighteen states known as the European Economic Area, effective from 1st January 1993.

The objective of the original six members of the Treaty of Rome was to remove barriers to trade and create a process leading to 'ever closer union' (preamble to the treaty); and this was to be achieved principally by 'establishing a common market and progressively approximating the economic policies of member states' (Article 2). In the words of Jean Monnet, architect of the Community, 'We are not creating an association of states: we are creating a union of peoples', and the administrative and decision-making procedures of the European Economic Community were accordingly structured so as to create a process leading towards the goal of political union.

This political purpose was re-affirmed in 1983 in the 'Stuttgart Solemn Declaration in favour of European Union'; and in 1986 in the Single European Act, member-states undertook 'to transform relations as a whole among their states into a European Union' (preamble), and stipulated that 'the European Communities and European Political Cooperation (i.e. harmonisation of foreign policies) would have as their objectives to contribute together to making concrete progress towards European Unity' (Article 1). A major provision of the Act designed to further the process of unification was the diminution of the blocking veto powers of individual member-governments by the extension of the system of qualified majority voting in the Council of Ministers.

The process of creating an economic involvement and dependence that would inevitably commit member states to a single political union was carried a major stage further in 1992 with the signing at Maastricht of the Treaty on European Union, which set as its objective the establishment of 'a European Union . . . a new stage in the process of creating an ever closer union among the peoples of Europe'. Provision was made for the Union to become a reality through, *inter alia*, the establishment of economic and monetary union, including the creation of a single currency, and the introduction of Union citizenship. Moreover, the Union would 'assert its identity in the international scene, in particular through the implementation of a common foreign and security policy'.

The Treaty, unlike the American Constitution, did not list in detail the functions that would be transferred to the Central Authority, on the assumption that the European Court of Justice would determine what responsibilities the Authority should assume in order to fulfil its agreed objective of creating the Union. However, it specified the goal of member states – namely a political union – and constituted a binding obligation to this end. It introduced a dynamic concept into the process of integration which would have a 'ratchet' effect, and it obliged governments to take further steps towards the goal of political union either as a Federation or as a Confederation. It constituted a source of Community Law, and an operative text. Together with the Treaty of Rome and the Single European Act (but providing no legal validity for the 1966 Luxembourg Agreement on majority voting procedure – 'the Luxembourg Compromise – which provides that member states are not bound to accept decisions of the European Council, where 'very important' national interests are at stake), the Maastricht Treaty formed the Constitution of the European Union. The European Court of Justice, in cases of doubt, will rule in favour of whatever measures promote integration, and will not necessarily limit its scope to its statutory functions.

Despite its immense legal complexity, the Treaty can be interpreted as creating three distinct structures: the European Community based on the rules and procedures of the three Treaties; the Common Foreign and Security policy envisaging the possibility of a European defence identity based on the Maastricht Treaty and subject to inter-governmental cooperation; and matters pertaining to justice and home affairs, also based on inter-governmental cooperation.

The three Treaties, together with their reassertion of previous commitments (the 'acquis communautaire'), form the Union's constitution. They are inevitably the result of competing national interest and differing interpretation, and will be subject to review at a Constitutional Conference to be held in 1996.

Since the signing of the Treaty of Rome an increasing degree of cooperation has taken place between the countries of Western Europe in general, and within the Community in particular, where a high degree of standardisation and conformity has been achieved in the fields of education, training, culture, transport coordination, food standards, competition and health and social policies. The Community's aim of establishing the 'Four Freedoms of Movement' – of goods, services, capital and people – has, in the main, been completed by the target date of January 1993, and non-tariff barriers to trade have been largely eliminated. Agriculture remains stubbornly within the orbit of politics rather than economics and will not be deregulated until the advent of a common currency; but substantial progress has been made in the transfer of resources and output-quotas from industrialised to agriculturally-dependent countries. Substantial progress had also been made in the transfer of resources to the less developed regions of the Community, thus reducing economic disequilibrium; whilst in the field of finance, the European Monetary System's exchange rate mechanism (ERM) has provided a valuable discipline for governments in the control of inflation, which was one of its objectives.

The ERM has not, however, succeeded in its aim of establishing exchange rate stability (stage I of EMS) as a precondition for the creation of the European Monetary Institute as from January 1994. The major tasks of the EMI are:

(a) to coordinate the activities of the Central Banks of member states and to bring about a levelling of their productive capacity i.e. 'economic convergence' (stage II);
(b) to bring about, by 1999, economic and monetary union (EMU), including the creation of a single currency and the centralised control of the economies of those member states which fulfil certain budgetary and national debt criteria as provided for in the Maastricht Treaty on European Union (stage III).

In 1992, after relatively minor readjustments within the ERM, the mechanism of mutual support broke down and the Pound Sterling and the Italian Lira were withdrawn from the system. Pressures had built up as a result of differences in economic policy and the slower-than-anticipated rate of economic convergence, and had been exacerbated by the maintenance of high interest rates in Germany – and consequently in the member states owing to their dependence on the Deutschmark – as a means of financing the unexpectedly high cost of German reunification. Moreover, the technological revolution in the money markets had enabled currency speculators and prudent bankers to transfer vast sums of money at the press of a button, thereby introducing a new factor into the process of exchange rate management.

In the field of joint foreign policy, members of the Community took a major initiative by recognising Croatia, Bosnia-Herzegovina and Slovenia (but not Macedonia) in 1992, and they have appointed a Commissioner for External Affairs. Various groups of member-states have also entered into agreements *à la carte* with the objective of furthering the process of integration e.g. the Schengen Group for the removal of frontier controls, the restructured Western European Union for combined defence, and the creation of a military force comprising units from Belgium, France, Germany and the Netherlands.

The institutions of the Community are:
*The Commission* of the European Communities which consists of seventeen members nominated by the governments of the member states but acting independently of them. (France, Germany, Italy, Spain and the United Kingdom nominate two members each, and the other countries one member each.) The Commission has the sole right of initiating measures to be adopted by the Community in those matters relating to the original European Economic Community; and in terms of the Treaty on European Union has the additional right, in conjunction with the Council of Ministers, of initiating proposals in the fields of foreign policy, security, justice and home affairs, e.g.

asylum, immigration and drugs. The Council of Ministers in some instances asks the Commission to initiate certain measures, which it will do if it sees fit. Each Commissioner is appointed by his member state for four years, and his responsibility for a particular function of the administration is allocated by the President of the Commission.

*The Council of the European Communities*, which consists of ministers nominated by, and representing, each of the twelve member states which considers and in certain limited instances can veto or amend proposals from the Commission. Decisions are in most cases to be taken by qualified (i.e. weighted) majority vote, but in some unanimity is required. When appropriate, the representatives on the Council are the Foreign Ministers, but according to the subjects of the agenda of each meeting may be the Ministers of agriculture, finance, transport, etc. The Presidency of the Council rotates every six months in alphabetical order. Whichever member has the Presidency presides also over all the various Council and committee meetings and determines their agenda, and its Foreign Minister delivers the opening speech to the European Parliament. Voting is weighted arbitrarily in terms of countries rather than democratically in terms of populations, the United Kingdom, France, Germany and Italy having ten votes, Spain eight, Belgium, the Netherlands, Greece and Portugal five, Ireland and Denmark three, and Luxembourg two.

*The European Parliament*, which consists of 567 members elected by direct franchise on the basis of ninety-nine members from Germany; eighty-seven each from France, Italy and the United Kingdom; sixty-four from Spain; thirty-one from the Netherlands; twenty-five each from Belgium, Greece and Portugal; sixteen from Denmark; fifteen from Ireland and six from Luxembourg. The Parliament has the right of consultation and discussion; it may propose changes in the Community Budget, amend it in certain details, or even reject it; and has the power to dismiss the Commission (something it has never done up till now). It has the power of co-decision with the Commission in matters regarding adhesion and association of new members, and effective blocking power mainly in matters regarding the internal market, and to some extent in matters of foreign policy and internal security.

*The Court of Justice*, which consists of thirteen independent judges, which is the Court in all matters relating to the Communities and the interpretation of the Community Treaties.

In addition to these four institutions:
*The European Council* was created at the summit meeting held in Paris in December 1984. It consists of the Heads of State or

of government of member states of the European Community accompanied by their Ministers for Foreign Affairs who meet at least twice a year, their main purpose being cooperation in a political context.

*The Committee of Permanent Representatives* (COREPER) consists of two committees: one of the Permanent Representatives (i.e. Ambassadors) of the member states accredited to the European Community, and the other comprising the deputy permanent representatives. Both meet every week and their main task is to process and prepare material for discussion and decision by the EC Council. They also carry out functions delegated by the Council.

*European Political Cooperation* (EPC) has increased steadily in importance, and although originally outside the legal framework of the European Communities it was institutionalised by the 1986 Single European Act. Like the European Council, it came into being as a result of an agreement between the member states, and its main aim is to harmonise and, where possible, coordinate the foreign policies of the respective member states.

A special relationship was established between members of the Community and their former dependent territories through the Yaoundé, Arusha and subsequently Lomé Conventions. The current convention (Lomé IV) runs from 1990–2000; its members are the twelve EC states and the sixty-nine ACP (Africa, Caribbean and Pacific) states, and it has a budget of 12,000 million ecus. Of this amount the European Development fund will provide 10,800 million ecus mainly in the form of grants for national and regional programmes, but also to compensate for losses in agricultural exports (STABEX) and to assist mining industries (SYSMIN). The European Investment Bank will provide 1,200 million ecus in the form of loans for specific projects. In terms of trade, the EC will provide duty-free access for nearly all ACP exports, and preferential prices for quotas of sugar and bananas. The institutions of the Convention are the ACP-EC Council of Ministers which meets annually, the ACP-EC Ambassadors Committee which meets every six months, and the EC-ACP, Joint Assembly composed of delegates of ACP countries and members of the European Parliament in equal numbers, which meets once a year. The ACP Secretariat is at 451 Ave. Georges Henri, Brussels.

# THE EUROPEAN ECONOMIC AREA

The EEA agreement was signed in 1992 and effective from 1 January 1993. It creates an area of Western Europe, which (with limited exceptions) ensures the free movement of industrial goods, capital, services and people: workers may accept offers of work and remain in any EEA country for this purpose; the self-employed are entitled to the right of establishment and to provide services, whilst students, pensioners and persons who are not economically active have the right of residence anywhere in the EEA. Joint EC/EFTA institutions are created, and the EFTA countries agree to accept relevant EC rules in such fields as competition, the environment, transport, capital movements, social policy, company law and consumer protection. The EEA consists of the eighteen member-states of the EC and EFTA: Austria, Belgium, Denmark, Finland, France, Germany, Greece, Iceland, Ireland, Italy, Liechtenstein, Luxembourg, the Netherlands, Norway, Portugal, Spain, Sweden, and the United Kingdom.

# EUROPEAN FREE TRADE ASSOCIATION

EFTA was founded in terms of the 1960 Stockholm Convention by seven Western European states which did not elect to join the EEC, with the principal objective of creating a free trade area in industrial goods, with agreed rules of origin. This was achieved in 1966, and in 1972/73 free trade agreements were concluded with the EC, creating the Western European Free Trade System. In 1992 agreement was reached between EFTA and EC member-states for the creation of the European Economic Area establishing a system (with certain exceptions) for the free movement of industrial goods, services, capital and people; and with the EFTA countries adopting relevant EC rules. The institutions of EFTA – the Council of Ministers, the Standing Committee, the Committee of Members of Parliament, the Consultative Committee and the Court – are supplemented by the creation of joint EFTA/EC institutions. Membership of EFTA is Austria, Finland, Iceland, Liechtenstein, Norway, Sweden and Switzerland, and the Secretariat-General is in Geneva.

# THE GULF COOPERATION COUNCIL

The Gulf Cooperation Council was founded in 1981 and its policy was set out in its Charter which was ratified in 1982. The member states are Bahrain, Kuwait, Oman, Qatar, Saudi Arabia and the United Arab Emirates. The essential purpose is to achieve coordination, cooperation and integration in all economic, social and cultural affairs, and considerable progress has been made in the face of external pressures. Comparable Regulations have been established in economic and financial affairs; commerce, customs and communication; education and culture; social and health affairs; media and tourism, and legislative and administrative affairs; whilst agreement has been reached on stimulating scientific and technological progress in industry, agriculture and water resources. In terms of The Unified Economic Agreement, tariff barriers between the six have been abolished, and Gulf nationals are free to set up industries and to enter into contracts in any state with equal rights. A Joint Defence Force for Rapid Deployment has also been formed.

The institutions of the Gulf Cooperation Council are the Supreme Council of Heads of State which meets annually, and the Council of Ministers which meets every three months; the Secretariat-General is in Riyadh, Saudi Arabia.

# INDIAN OCEAN COMMISSION

The members of the Indian Ocean Commission are Comoro, Madagascar, Mauritius, Seychelles and France acting on behalf of Réunion and being represented by the Préfet of the island. Regular meetings of Foreign Ministers are held, as well as Meetings of Experts from time to time. The object of the Commission is to foster cooperation and the resolution of common problems among the countries of the South-West Indian Ocean on the basis of the Agreement signed in January 1984. The Chairmanship rotates between member countries, and there is no fixed Secretariat.

# ISLAMIC CONFERENCE ORGANISATION

The Islamic Conference Organisation was founded in 1971 and consists of forty-six member states together with Zanzibar. Its aim is the promotion of Islamic interests and solidarity in all their aspects, based on the Declaration of Lahore of 1974 which confirmed the full national rights of the Palestinian people in their homeland, the decision of the 1975 conference to establish a permanent committee (the Al-Quds Committee) to pursue the question of the future of

Jerusalem, and the Casablanca Charter of 14 January 1984 which established committees for regional reconciliation and concord to settle differences between members.

The ICO has maintained an active and consistent role in international relations, exemplified by the Mecca Declaration of 28 January 1979 concerning Afghanistan, and the efforts since 1982 to mediate in the Gulf. Conferences of Heads of State take place annually, and meetings of Foreign Ministers take place annually or more often as circumstances demand. Of the various subsidiary organisations, the Committee on Economic Affairs seeks to promote mutual economic cooperation and solidarity among Moslem countries.

## LATIN AMERICAN ECONOMIC ORGANISATIONS

*The Latin American Integration Association* (LAIA or ALADI) was established in 1980 by the new Treaty of Montevideo, which superseded the 1960 Treaty which created the Latin American Free Trade Area (LAFTA). The purpose of the new treaty is to pursue the integration process in order to promote the harmonious and balanced socio-economic development of the region; the long-term objective of such a process is the gradual and progressive establishment of a Latin American common market (article I). The scope of the new treaty is greater than that of the original one, but the methods of achieving closer cooperation are more flexible, and in the form of a framework for pragmatic development, rather than a fixed timetable for achieving specific objectives. The treaty makes provision for regional tariff preferences, regional and sub-regional cooperational agreements, assistance to less developed member states, and the establishment of relations with other regional economic organisation. The Secretariat is in Montevideo, and the member states are the same as for the previous treaty, namely Argentina, Bolivia, Brasil, Chile, Columbia, Ecuador, Mexico, Paraguay, Peru, Uruguay and Venezuela. Policy is determined by the Council of Ministers of Foreign Affairs of each of the member countries which meets when appropriate, whilst the Committee of Representatives is the permanent executive body.

Complementary organisations are the *Sistema Económico Latino-americano* (SELA) which meets at intervals in order to coordinate economic planning and policies and whose membership includes nearly all Latin American countries; and the *United Nations Economic Commission for Latin America and the Caribbean* which is a

111

centre for economic research, and a source of economic and social information. The seat of the Commission is Santiago, Chile.

*The Andean Group* (Grupo Andino) was formed in 1969 by Bolivia, Chile, Ecuador and Peru (and subsequently Venezuela) as a sub-regional economic group with the objective of creating a more cohesive and effective economic unit within the Latin American Free Trade Area, particularly relating to foreign investment (decision 24 of the Cartagena Agreement). Chile subsequently withdrew from the organisation.

# MERCOSUR: THE SOUTHERN CONE COMMON MARKET

MERCOSUR was established in 1991 by the Treaty of Asunción for the purposes of establishing a Customs Union including goods, services, capital and labour, and for promoting regional investment. Member-states are Argentina, Brasil, Paraguay and Uruguay.

# NORTH ATLANTIC TREATY ORGANISATION

When Mr Arabatov, adviser to Mr Gorbachev, said in 1989 'we are going to do something terrible to you, we are going to deprive you of your enemy' he could well have been addressing himself to NATO, whose task it had been, since 1949, to deter, contain and if necessary defeat that enemy.

The essence of the North Atlantic Treaty is that an armed attack against one or more of the signatories is considered as an attack against them all. The area of application of the treaty extends to the territory of any of the parties in Europe and North America; an attack on the forces of any party in Europe, on the islands under the jurisdiction of any party in the North Atlantic area north of the Tropic of Cancer, or on the vessels or aircraft of any of the parties in this area.

The prime concern of NATO, acting in a defensive capacity, continues to be to safeguard the security, sovereignty and territorial integrity of its members, maintaining security at the lowest possible level of forces consistent with the requirements of defence. It will continue consultations on current political developments and will seek, through dialogue, partnership and cooperation, a new and more peaceful order, based on the conviction that stability and security in the Euro-Atlantic area will increasingly be built on a framework of interlocking and mutually reinforcing institutions: NATO, the CSCE, the European Community, the Western European Union and the Council of Europe. Moreover, in response to the changed political and military situation in Europe, the member countries of NATO, together with Bulgaria, the then Czechoslovakia, Estonia, Hungary, Latvia, Lithuania, Poland, Romania and the then Soviet Union agreed in December 1991 to create the North Atlantic Cooperation Council. The institutions of the Council are annual meetings at Ministerial level; bimonthly meetings at Ambassadorial level, and *ad hoc* meetings as circumstances may require. The major concern of the Council is security and related matters, in particular the implementation of the Treaty on the Non-Proliferation of Nuclear Weapons; preventing the unauthorised export of nuclear or other destabilising military technologies, and the problem of converting defence production to civilian purposes.

Members of the Alliance are Belgium, Canada, Denmark, Germany, Greece, Iceland, Italy, Luxembourg, the Netherlands, Norway, Portugal, Spain, Turkey and the United Kingdom. France was an original signatory of the treaty, but withdrew from the integrated military organisation, (but not the civil organisation) in 1966. Meetings of the North Atlantic Cooperation Council normally take place at the NATO Secretariat, which is situated in Brussels.

# NORTH AMERICAN FREE TRADE AGREEMENT

NAFTA, signed in 1992 by Canada, Mexico and the United States of America, establishes a Free Trade Area by the phased removal of tariffs and quotas on industrial and agricultural good in the area, and by freedom to establish services.

# ORGANISATION FOR ECONOMIC COOPERATION AND DEVELOPMENT

The OECD was established as a successor to the Organisation for European Economic Cooperation (OEEC) and came into being on 30 September 1961. Its objectives are to promote economic and social welfare throughout the OECD area by assisting its member Governments in the formulation of policies designed to this end, and by coordinating these policies; and to stimulate and harmonise its members' aid efforts in favour of developing countries. The supreme body of the Organisation is the Council, composed of one representative from each member country. It meets at permanent representative (normally ambassadorial) level approximately once a week under the chairmanship of the Secretary-General, and at ministerial level usually once a year under the chairmanship of a Minister elected annually. Decisions and Recommendations are adopted by mutual agreement of all members of the Council. The Council is assisted by an Executive Committee composed of fourteen members of the Council designated annually by the latter.

The major part of the Organisation's work is prepared and carried out in specialised committees and working parties of which there are about 200. These include Committees for Economic Policy; Economic and Development Review; Development Assistance-(DAC); Trade; Invisible Transactions; Financial Markets; Fiscal-Affairs; Restrictive Business Practices; Consumer Policy; Tourism; Maritime Transport; International Investment and Multi-national Enterprises; Energy Policy; Industry; Steel; Scientific and Technological Policy; Education; Manpower and Social Affairs; Environment; Agriculture; Fisheries, etc.

Four autonomous or semi-autonomous bodies also belong to the Organisation: the International Energy Agency (IEA); the Nuclear Energy Agency (NEA); the Development Centre; and the Centre for Educational Research and Innovation. In 1990 the Centre for Cooperation with the European Economics in Transition (CCEET) was established to act as the point of contact between the OECD and central and eastern European countries seeking guidance in moving towards a market economy.

Members of OECD are Australia, Austria, Belgium, Canada, Denmark, Finland, France, Germany, Greece, Iceland, Ireland, Italy, Japan, Luxembourg, the Netherlands, New Zealand, Norway, Portugal, Spain, Sweden, Switzerland, Turkey, the United Kingdom and the United States. The Commission of the European Community generally takes part in the work of OECD. The secretariat, headed by the Secretary-General, is in Paris.

# ORGANISATION OF AFRICAN UNITY

The OAU is an organisation of independent African States based on the Organisation's Charter, signed by member states in Addis Ababa on 25 May 1963.

The main objectives of the Organisation are to promote the unity and solidarity of African states; to coordinate and intensify their cooperation and efforts to achieve a better life for the peoples of Africa; to defend their sovereignty, their territorial integrity and independence; to eradicate all forms of colonialism from Africa; and to promote international cooperation having due regard to the Charter of the United Nations and the Universal Declaration of Human Rights.

The principal institutions of the Organisation are the Assembly of Heads of State and Government, the supreme policy-making body which meets at least once a year; the Council of Ministers which meets at least twice a year; the General Secretariat of the Organisation situated in Addis Ababa and headed by a Secretary-General appointed by the Assembly; the Commission of Mediation, Conciliation and Arbitration consisting of twenty-one members, established by a Protocol signed by OAU member states in Cairo on 21 July 1964; the Coordinating Committee for the Liberation Movements of Africa situated in Dar es Salaam, and eight Specialised Commissions.

# ORGANISATION OF AMERICAN STATES

The OAS has inherited a long tradition of cooperation in North, Central and South America and is today the supreme regional coordinating body for all matters affecting interstate relations in this region. It is based on the 1948 Charter of the Organisation of American States as amended by the 1967 Protocol of Buenos Aires and the 1985 Protocol of Cartagena de Indias. The members of the Organisation are: Antigua and Barbuda, Argentina, Bahamas, Barbados, Belize, Bolivia, Brasil, Canada, Chile, Columbia, Costa Rica, Cuba, Dominica, Dominican Republic, Ecuador, El Salvador, Grenada, Guatemala, Guyana, Haiti, Honduras, Jamaica, Mexico, Nicaragua, Panama, Paraguay, Peru, Saint Christopher and Nevis, St Lucia, St Vincent and the Grenadines, Suriname, Trinidad and Tobago, the United States of America, Uruguay and Venezuela. Policy matters are determined by the General Assembly which meets annually and in occasional special sessions, and Consultative Meetings of Ministers of Foreign Affairs which are held when necessary. Three Councils, each composed of one representative of each member state, meet in Washington, where the General Secretariat is situated. These are the Permanent Council which supervises the work of the Organisation and deals with matters of political nature; the Inter-American Economic and Social Council; and the Inter-American Council for Education, Science and Culture. In addition, there are the Inter-American Judicial Committee and the Inter-American Commission on Human Rights.

# ORGANISATION OF THE PETROLEUM EXPORTING COUNTRIES

OPEC was founded in 1960 by Iran, Iraq, Kuwait, Saudi Arabia and Venezuela in order to harmonise petroleum policies and to protect the interests of members states. Subsequently Algeria, Gabon, Indonesia, Libya, Nigeria, Qatar and the United Arab Emirates joined, and Venezuela withdrew from, the Organisation. OPEC's pricing policies have a considerable influence on those of most other oil-exporting countries. Regular meetings of OPEC Oil Ministers are held at intervals of six months, with provision for extraordinary meetings. The Secretariat of OPEC is in Vienna.

# PREFERENTIAL TARIFF AREA

This is a group of nineteen East and Central African countries seeking to promote free trade. The Secretariat is in Lusaka.

# SOUTH ASIAN ASSOCIATION FOR REGIONAL COOPERATION

The South Asian Association for Regional Cooperation comprising Bangladesh, Bhutan, India, Maldives, Nepal, Pakistan and Sri Lanka was inaugurated at the first Summit meeting of the Heads of State and Heads of Government of the seven South Asian countries held in Dhaka, Bangladesh, in December 1985.

Organisationally SAARC has four tiers. At the lowest level is the Technical Committee, which in a specified area of cooperation formulates programmes, determines their financial implications, implements them and monitors their progress. The second is the Standing Committee of Foreign Secretaries of member countries which reviews and coordinates the work of the Technical Committees, and identifies new areas of cooperation. It meets at least once a year. Political sanction for the work of the Standing Committee is given by the Foreign Ministers who form the third tier, also meeting once a year. The fourth organisational level is the Summit, which gives full political significance to SAARC. Decisions at all levels are taken on the basis of unanimity; bilateral and contentious issues are excluded from SAARC deliberations; regional cooperation is not held as a substitute for bilateral or multilateral cooperation, but as complementary to them; cooperation is based on respect for the principles of sovereign equality, territorial integrity, political independence, and non-interference in the internal affairs of other states.

The launching of SAARC in December 1985 set in motion a process of regional cooperation, active collaboration and mutual assistance among the countries of the South Asian region in the economic, cultural, technological and scientific fields. It also highlights the objective of strengthening cooperation in international forums on matters of common interest and of enhancing mutual trust, understanding and appreciation of one another's problems between the seven member states which jointly account for one billion people or roughly one-fifth of the human race.

A permanent Secretariat of SAARC is yet to be established.

# SOUTH PACIFIC REGIONAL ORGANISATIONS

*The South Pacific Bureau for Economic Cooperation* (SPEC) is the major regional organisation in the South Pacific with its Secretariat in Suva, Fiji. It concerns itself with a wide range of economic matters relating to cooperation within the South Pacific region, and equally with the region's external relations: in particular commodity marketing, industrial development, tourism, shipping, civil aviation, transfer of technology, oil prospecting and environmental protection.

*The South Pacific Forum* (SPF) is restricted to sovereign states in the South Pacific, including Australia and New Zealand. It consists of an annual meeting of Heads of Governments at which political, as well as economic, matters are discussed. The Secretariat is provided by SPEC.

*The South Pacific Commission* (SPC) is concerned principally with rural development, youth and community development, *ad hoc* expert consultancies, cultural exchanges, training facilities and marine resource development and research. It consists of twenty-seven sovereign states and self-governing territories in the South Pacific including Australia and New Zealand, the United Kingdom and the United States of America. The Secretariat is in Noumeia, New Caledonia.

*The Single Regional Organisation* (SRO) is a proposal under deliberation with a view to creating a single body to serve the social, cultural and economic development interests of all the Pacific Islands.

# SOUTHERN AFRICAN DEVELOPMENT COMMUNITY

The SADC was established by Treaty in 1992 in order to promote closer economic cooperation and to foster collaboration in fields of mutual interest. Member-states are Angola, Botswana, Lesotho, Malawi, Mozambique, Namibia, Swaziland, Tanzania, Zambia and Zimbabwe.

# VISEGRÁD GROUP

A regional organisation for the coordination of mutual interests, the members are the Czech Republic, Hungary, Poland and Slovakia.

# WEST AFRICAN INTERGOVERNMENTAL ECONOMIC GROUPINGS

There are over thirty intergovernmental economic groupings in West Africa. To a large extent they are the product of the historical differences within the region, and most have the same objectives of economic harmonisation and eventual integration. The most important are:

*The Economic Community of West African States*, was created at Lagos on the 28 May 1975 to promote economic development in West Africa by establishing a common market (based on the progressive elimination of all discriminations between national boundaries) and harmonising a variety of economic policies including agricultural policies, industrial development plans and monetary policies, co-operation for the development of energy and mineral resources and for the joint development of infrastructure. In addition it has accepted responsibility for organising military peace-keeping forces in the area. ECOWAS is the all-embracing economic integration grouping in West Africa since of its sixteen members, five are officially anglophone (The Gambia, Ghana, Liberia, Nigeria, Sierra Leone); eight francophone (Benin, Burkina Faso, Côte d'Ivoire, Guinea, Mali, Niger, Senegal, Togo); two Lusophone (Cape Verde and Guinea Bissau), and one arabic-speaking (Mauritania).

*The Council of the Entente States*, is one of the oldest groupings, founded in 1959 by Benin, Burkina Faso, and Côte d'Ivoire and joined by Togo on 3 June 1966. It is an informal instrument for the coordination of economic policies among member states, and has a Mutual Aid and Guarantee Fund for economic cooperation.

*The Mano River Union* (MRU), was established by Liberia and Sierra Leone in October 1973, and joined by Guinea in October 1980. Its objectives are the establishment of a customs union and the expansion of trade by the elimination of all barriers to mutual trade, the creation of conditions favourable to an expansion of mutual productive capacity, cooperation in the creation of new productive capacity and the security of a fair distribution of the benefits from economic cooperation.

*The River Niger Commission or the River Niger Basin Authority* (RNC), was established in October 1983 by Benin, Burkina Faso, Cameroon, Côte d'Ivoire, Mali, Niger and Nigeria for promoting, encouraging and coordinating studies and programmes related to the development of the Niger Basin.

*The Organisation for the Development of the Senegal River* (OMVS), was established in 1972 in Nouakchott by Mali, Mauritania and Senegal, and is open to all states through which the river flows provided that they accept the spirit and letter of the Convention.

*The West African Clearing House* (WACH), comprising Benin, Burkina Faso, Côte d'Ivoire, The Gambia, Ghana, Liberia, Mali, Niger, Nigeria, Senegal, and Sierra Leone, was established in 1975 in Freetown to promote the use of the currencies of member states for intra-regional trade and other transactions, to bring about economies in the use of the members' foreign currency reserves, to encourage the members to liberalise trade among themselves and to promote monetary cooperation and consultation.

*The Economic Community of West Africa* (CEAO), together with its financial institutions: the West African Monetary Union (UMOA) whose central bank, the Banque Centrale des Etats de l'Afrique de l'Ouest (BCEAO) issues a common currency tied to the French franc. The CEAO consists of the francophone West African States of Benin, Burkina Faso, Côte D'Ivoire, Mali, Mauritania, Niger and Senegal, and the aim is regional economic cooperation for their development through free trade in products of local origin (such as livestock, agricultural products, fish and mineral products) that have not undergone industrial processing (i.e. raw materials); a special preferential import duty regime, (the regional cooperation tax) for traded manufactured products that originate in member states; and the establishment of a common external tariff.

# WESTERN EUROPEAN UNION

The origins of the Western European Union can be traced back to the 1948 Brussels Treaty between Belgium, France, Luxembourg, the Netherlands and the United Kingdom providing for collective self-defence, mutual automatic military assistance in the event of hostilities and for collaboration in economic, social and cultural matters. Germany, Greece, Italy, Portugal and Spain subsequently acceded; Turkey, Norway and Iceland are associates, and Ireland and Denmark have observer status. After exercising various functions in the political evolution of Western Europe and providing a forum for the coordination on policies of international concern, the members agreed to revise their structure with the establishment of three Agencies, as from 1 January 1986. Their tasks, in addition to those assumed in connection with the evolution of the European Community, are:

- The study of arms control and disarmament questions (Agency I).
- The study of security and defence questions (Agency II).
- The development of cooperation in the field of armaments (Agency III).

Policy making rests with the Council of Ministers, served by the Secretary-General located in Brussels, whilst the Assembly of the WEU meets twice a year.

*Chapter 9*

# INTERNATIONAL LAW AND PRACTICE

## DEFINITION AND GENERAL PRINCIPLES

International law is the outcome of man's endeavours to extend into the field of interstate relations the rule of order and the respect for law which exists within the state. The period since the end of the Cold War, however, has not been an encouraging one for its advocates. Whether in the field of recognition, extradition or the use of force, international law has been ignored, contravened or perhaps worse, abused in the political interest.

Basically – and traditionally – international law is defined as the body of rules governing the relations between states. However, since the rapid evolution of the concepts of social and interstate responsibilities resulting from postwar factors and events (e.g. the creation of new states and increased involvement of the individual) and reflected in the development of the United Nations, a wider definition of the term has become necessary. The following is J. G. Starke's definition as contained in his *Introduction to International Law*.

International law may be defined as that body of law which is composed for its greater part of the principles and rules of conduct which states feel themselves bound to observe, and therefore, do commonly observe in their relations with each other, and which include also:

(a) the rules of law relating to the functioning of international institutions or organisations, their relations with each other and their relations with states and individuals; and

(b) certain rules of law relating to individuals and non-state entities so far as the rights or duties of such individuals and non-state entities are the concern of the international community.

Although international law is the subject of much debate and opposing viewpoints, there are certain areas of almost complete agreement (e.g. piracy on the high seas and the immunities of diplomats), just as at the other end of the spectrum there are areas of considerable disagreement. It cannot thus be claimed that it is a subject merely for academic lawyers; but on the other hand it could be argued that 'international law' was, in some respects, a contradiction in terms. It is something of a paradox, attracting both disciples and sceptics: those who, with missionary zeal, see it as the path to world peace and righteousness; and those who maintain that without legislature or international sanctions there can be no international law. Both views are to some extent valid, and its relevance in diplomatic relations lies in the fact that considerations of international law do in fact influence governments and provide standards of international behaviour which they acknowledge as being the ideal, even though they may not always manage to live up to them. But like all good causes, international law is liable to be the subject of evil designs, and politicians the world over are not slow to invoke and if necessary distort its principles when it suits their purposes, or to disclaim them if they should prove to be embarrassing. It is thus a subject that diplomats must be acquainted with, but handle with care. The sources of international law are, in brief: treaties, custom, general principles of law, judicial precedents and the writings of leading authorities.

The following topics have been selected as being of interest to diplomats and as a basis for further study; it is not pretended that issues of international law can be effectively reduced to simple generalisations and to imprecise non-legal terminology.

# TREATIES AND TREATY-MAKING

## GENERAL PRINCIPLES

States enter into treaty relationships when they agree with each other or with a group of other states to undertake certain commitments. Treaties invariably take the form of documents, though a verbal undertaking could be claimed to have the same validity as a written one.

Treaties (to use the general term) may be made in different forms, such as between Heads of State; between states; between governments (to some extent in the order of their importance and formality, but often depending on whim or custom). Such treaties are equally binding on the states concerned even though they may be expressed to be agreements between Heads of State or governments.

## TYPES OF TREATIES

The instruments recording international agreements have various titles: agreement, arrangement, convention, declaration, exchange of notes, general act, *modus vivendi, procès-verbale*, protocol, or statute. All have equal validity but vary in form and wording; and as far as practice in the USA is concerned ratification by the Senate is required for treaties, but agreements can be concluded either following Congressional approval or upon constitutional authority. Generally speaking, bilateral instruments take the form of a treaty, agreement, exchange of notes or *modus vivendi* (in the order of their importance and formality); and multilateral instruments take the form of treaty or convention unless they are on a grand scale when such terms as general act or statute apply. A Final Act is a series of agreements or treaties resulting from a conference, each one of which requires specific approval.

A *protocol of signature*, which is rarely used, has a particular function in that it may be used as a sort of 'postscript' to a treaty. It is considered by the negotiators to be part of the treaty but is written and signed as a separate document. It is less formal than the treaty it accompanies and may record reservations by certain signatories, clarification of points in the treaty, or other subsidiary considerations. It may be used after a short period to record a further point of agreement.

A *'Protocol'*, which is often used, is an international agreement that is usually supplementary to, or amends, a treaty. An *exchange of letters* may be attached to a treaty for roughly similar purposes, but these are a rather less formal record of intentions and are not necessarily signed by the negotiators. However, an *exchange of notes* (or letters) is more normally made independently of a treaty, as a less formal means of recording agreement between states.

## THE PROCESS OF TREATY-MAKING

### (a) Accreditation and full powers

The process of treaty-making requires that the persons who conduct the negotiations on behalf of the states concerned should be able to prove that they are authorised to do so; that is to say that they should

123

be able to produce their *credentials*. These usually take the form of a letter signed by or on behalf of the Minister for Foreign Affairs.

If a treaty or other international instrument is to be concluded and signed at bilateral negotiations or at a multilateral conference, representatives (unless, for example, they are heads of government or Ministers for Foreign Affairs) must be provided with *full powers*. (If the treaty is between Heads of State the full powers are signed by the Head of State; if between governments, by the Minister for Foreign Affairs.)

A typical example of full powers issued to a delegate to a plenipotentiary conference would be as follows:

> Whereas, for the better treating of and arranging certain matters which may come into discussion between the Government of . . . and the Governments of certain other Powers and States represented at the forthcoming Conference [name of Conference] to be held at . . . on . . . it is expedient that a fit person should be invested with Full Power to conduct the said discussion on the part of the Government of . . . : I, [name in full] Minister for Foreign Affairs, do hereby certify that
>
> [name in full, decorations and official designation of the leader of the delegation]
>
> is by these Presents named, constituted and appointed as Plenipotentiary and Representative having Full Power and Authority to agree and conclude with such Plenipotentiaries and Representatives as may be vested with similar Power and Authority on the part of the Governments aforesaid any Treaty, Convention, Agreement, Protocol or other Instrument that may tend to the attainment of the above-mentioned end, and to sign for the Government of . . . everything so agreed upon and concluded. Further, I do hereby certify that whatever things shall be so transacted and concluded by the said Plenipotentiary and Representative shall, subject if necessary to Ratification by the Government of . . . be agreed to, acknowledged and accepted by the said Government of . . . in the fullest manner.
>
> In witness whereof I have signed these Presents and affixed hereto my Seal.
>
> Signed and sealed at the Ministry of Foreign Affairs (place) . . . the . . . day of . . . One thousand Nine hundred and ninety . . .
>
> *Seal*                                        Signature of Minister
>                                                for Foreign Affairs

At conferences in which a large number of states are participating, it is customary for a Credentials or a Full Powers Committee to be established for the purpose of confirming the powers and authenticity of the delegates.

### (b) Negotiation

The negotiation of a treaty is normally preceded by an understanding between the states concerned – sometimes a *letter of intent* – as to the general purpose and likely outcome of its proceedings. In the case of multilateral negotiations an *agenda* is usually agreed in advance. In the case of a bilateral treaties it is usual for the governments to outline the pattern of negotiations and subdivide them under specific *heads of agreement*. It may then be found advisable to refer certain heads to technical or specialist subcommittees so that their conclusions can be considered by the negotiators at a plenary session. The art of negotiation needs no elaboration: it is the skill and patience of the marketplace elevated to a higher plane. Negotiators, however, are usually limited in their conduct by written instructions from their government – their 'brief' – and by the availability of the telephone or fax which enables them to refer back all major problems for decision.

### (c) Authentication and signature of the text

When a document has been agreed it is either initialled, signed, or signed *ad referendum* by the negotiating representatives. Initialling normally signifies merely the establishment of an authentic text, and further action is required to signify the consent of the states to be bound. Signature *ad referendum* requires confirmation by the state concerned to constitute full signature. If the treaty is 'subject to ratification', signature is of limited significance. In other cases, whether the signature of the properly accredited delegate makes the treaty binding on his state or not depends on the intention as shown by the terms of the treaty, e.g. with regard to its entry into force; as agreed during the negotiations, or as otherwise indicated, e.g. by the terms of the relevant full powers. Multilateral treaties may in most instances be signed with reservations if these are not excluded by the terms of the treaty or incompatible with its object and purpose.

### (d) Ratification

Where ratification is stipulated (or understood) a treaty is referred to the governments of the negotiating parties for confirmation. Ratification in the international law sense is an executive act: whether or not this is effected before the national legislature gives it approval or legislates to implement the treaty being a matter of domestic law and practice. A state is under no legal obligation to ratify a treaty agreed by its own delegate, but its choice of action is limited to acceptance or complete rejection though in exceptional cases, ratification may be made with reservations, these being usually of a procedural rather than substantive nature. It cannot normally ask to re-open negotiations with a view to introducing amendments. Ratification is not retroactive to the date of the signature of the treaty (unless special provision is made to this effect). The constitution of the USA provides that the ratification of all international treaties must be approved by a two-thirds majority of the Senate.

*(e) Acceptance*
In some instances provision may be made for the 'acceptance' of treaties as an alternative to ratification, accession or adherence. The practice is a new one, intended to meet constitutional difficulties of certain states; it mainly relates to United Nations Conventions, some of which contain an acceptance formula clause. Acceptance is effected by the deposit of an instrument of acceptance.

*(f) Accession or adherence*
Provision may be made in treaties (normally multilateral) for subsequent accession or adherence (occasionally adhesion) by states which did not originally sign the treaty. The two terms are generally considered to be synonymous, but it is sometimes held that 'accession' is used to apply to the whole treaty, and 'adherence' to only part of it. Accession or adherence can take place only with the consent of all signatories of the treaty, and where it is considered to be acceptable a permissive clause to this effect is usually included in the treaty.

*(g) Exchange or deposit of ratifications*
The signature of an instrument of ratification on behalf of a state has in itself little significance in international law; it is only the exchange of instruments of ratification that gives them effect – or, as is usual in the case of multilateral conventions, their being deposited with the depositary. (The depositary may be a government or the secretariat of an organisation.) The exchange or deposit of ratification is usually effected and recorded by means of a *procès-verbale*. Instruments of ratification are signed by the Head of State, by the head of government or by the Minister for Foreign Affairs, depending on the importance of the issue.

*(h) Registration and publication*
Article 102 of the United Nations Charter stipulates that all treaties and international agreements entered into by member states shall be registered with the Secretariat and published by them. Failure to do so (on either part) does not invalidate the treaty; but it has the consequence that the treaty may not be invoked before the International Court of Justice or any other organ of the United Nations.

## THE FORM AND CONTENT OF TREATIES

Treaties can normally be divided into three parts:

1. *The preamble*, somewhat formal in style, setting out the names of the parties to the agreement, the names of the plenipotentiaries and the object of the agreement, e.g.

'The Republic of X and the Kingdom of Y
Desiring to facilitate .........................................................
Having in mind .................................................................
Having resolved to conclude a Treaty of ...............................
and have appointed as their Plenipotentiaries for this purpose:

The Republic of X: The Hon. A.B.C.
The Kingdom of Y: His Excellency D.E.F.

Who, having communicated their respective full powers, found in good and due form, have agreed as follows . . .'

2. *The terms or substance of the agreement*, known as the substantive clauses.

3. *The administrative clauses* or final clauses (sometimes known as the *clauses protocolaires*) which include provision for some or all of the following:

The date or method of entry into force of the treaty
The duration and method of termination of the treaty
Definition of terms
The method of settlement of any dispute
Reservations
Accession to the treaty by other states
Amendment or review
The languages of the treaty which are to be authoritative
Ratification, and deposit of instruments of ratification
Registration with the United Nations
and invariably:

Date and place of signature
Signature (and sometimes seal) or plenipotentiaries.

## THE VALIDITY OF TREATIES

A treaty is essentially a contract between states, and its validity may theoretically be challenged by one or more of the parties concerned on various grounds, which are specified in Articles 48–53 of the Vienna Convention on the Law of Treaties. These are:

*Error* relating to a fact or situation which was assumed by the state concerned to exist at the time when the treaty was concluded and which formed an essential basis of its consent to be bound by the treaty (except if that state contributed by its own conduct to the error or if the circumstances were such as to put the state on notice of a possible error).

*Fraud*, i.e. when a state has been induced to conclude a treaty by the fraudulent conduct of another negotiating state.

*Corruption of a representative* of a state.

*Coercion of a representative* of a state.

*Coercion of a state* by the threat or use of force.

*Jus cogens*: i.e. treaties conflicting with a peremptory norm of general international law. A 'peremptory norm' in this context is one accepted and recognised by the international community of states as a whole as a norm from which no derogation is permitted and which can be modified only by a subsequent norm of general international law having the same character.

No general rule can be given to cover the case where a treaty which is signed in good faith proves to be incompatible with the terms of an earlier treaty – a situation capable of arising as between a bilateral agreement and a multilateral agreement possibly through the oversight of an archivist. So far as the provisions of the United Nations Charter are concerned, article 103 stipulates that obligations under the Charter shall have precedence over all others in the event of conflict.

## THE TERMINATION OF TREATIES

A treaty may legitimately come to an end by the agreement of the parties concerned; at the expiry of the time limit provided in the treaty, or by parties making use of a termination clause provided in the treaty. In the absence of any of these provisions it may (in practice though doubtfully in law) be unilaterally abrogated or denounced if the party concerned considers that the political consequences (if any) of so doing would be less onerous than the maintenance of the provisions of the treaty. Varying degrees of legitimacy can be claimed for such unilateral action in the event of:

(a) a fundamental change having taken place in the circumstances which existed at the time the treaty was drawn up;

(b) the extinction of the other contracting party as a state (in a bilateral treaty) in such a way that the successor state does not inherit rights or obligations under this treaty;
(c) the out-break of war;
(d) the denunciation of a multilateral treaty by such a number of the parties as to render the treaty inoperative;
(e) a material breach of the treaty by another party to it.

# POLITICAL ASYLUM AND THE EXTRADITION OF CRIMINALS

There are two categories of political asylum: *territorial asylum* (i.e. granted by a state to an alien in its territory) and *extra-territorial* or *diplomatic asylum* (i.e. in the premises of a diplomatic mission or other such premises entitled to inviolability). Instances of the former are many, and groups of 'political refugees' are to be found in most states; but because they are living in a different country they are no great embarrassment to their own government.

A different situation arises in instances of diplomatic asylum, when the political offender is able to live protected and unmolested in his own country and in the midst of his fellow-countrymen whom he is presumably attempting to turn against their government.

As a general principle, a state has the right to grant asylum to aliens within its own territory ('territorial asylum'), and the onus is on the state wishing to extradite them to show why they should be given up. If on the other hand a state has given refuge in one of its missions to a national of the state in which it is situated ('extra-territorial asylum') it is up to the head of that mission, or his government, to justify the action.

Special provision relating to, *inter alia*, extradition has been made in respect of crimes against internationally protected persons in the United Nations Convention on the Prevention and Punishment of Crimes against Internationally Protected Persons, including Diplomatic Agents of 14 December 1973 (the New York Convention).

## DIPLOMATIC ASYLUM

The inviolability of the premises of a diplomatic mission has traditionally rendered them liable to be sought as a place of refuge. The question of the existence and validity of this right of asylum from political persecution (it is not normally applicable in ordinary criminal cases) remains dormant for long periods, only to be the subject of acrimonious discussion from time to time. In Europe the practice is nearly extinct. It is a situation that can, in the end, be resolved only by negotiation, if only because the Vienna Convention on Diplomatic Relations, whilst ensuring the inviolability of the premises of a diplomatic mission (and thus of those within it) makes no provision for the departure under safe conduct of any person not covered by the Convention. In other regions, local usage sanctions its continuation even though diplomatic asylum is not recognised as existing in terms of Customary International Law. The Latin American practice may be summarised on the basis of the Convention on Diplomatic Asylum drawn up by the Tenth Inter-American Conference held in Caracas in 1954, as follows:

1. Every state has the right to grant asylum, and to determine for itself the nature of the offence or the motives for the persecution of the person seeking asylum.
2. In the context of the granting of asylum, a legation includes not only the seat of a regular diplomatic mission and the residence of the head of mission, but also any other premises provided by the mission for the asylees when their number exceeds the normal capacity of the buildings.
3. Asylum may not be granted except in urgent cases and for the period of time strictly necessary for the asylee to depart from the country with the guarantees granted by the government of the territorial state.
4. Urgent cases are understood to be those, among others, in which the individual is being sought by persons or mobs over whom the authorities have lost control, or by the authorities themselves, and is in danger of being deprived of his life or liberty because of political persecution and cannot, without risk, ensure his safety in any other way. It shall rest with the state granting asylum to determine the degree of urgency of the case.
5. It is not lawful to grant asylum to persons who, at the time of requesting it, are under indictment or on trial for common offences or have been convicted by competent regular courts and have not served the respective sentence, nor to deserters from land, sea, and air forces, save when the acts giving rise to the request for asylum are clearly of a political nature.
6. Immediately asylum is granted the fact must be reported to the Minister for Foreign Affairs of the state of the person who has secured asylum, or to the local administrative authorities if the act occurred outside the capital.
7. The government of the state has the right to require that the asylee be sent out of the national territory within the shortest

possible time; and the diplomatic agent of the country which has granted asylum in turn has the right to require that the asylee be permitted to leave the territory; and in both instances the necessary guarantee of safe conduct and inviolability must be provided.

8. Asylees enjoying safe conduct may not be deposited at any point in or near the national territory from which they have sought asylum.
9. While enjoying asylum, refugees shall not be allowed to perform acts contrary to the public peace.
10. If, as a consequence of a rupture of diplomatic relations, the diplomatic representative who granted asylum has to leave the territorial state, he must be allowed to leave with the asylees, or if this is not possible, he may surrender them to the diplomatic mission of a third state.
11. The fact that the government of the territorial state is not recognised by the state granting asylum does not prejudice the application of the general principles set out above; nor does their application imply recognition.

## EXTRADITION

Extradition is the forcible removal of a person from one state to another to stand trial or suffer imprisonment for an alleged offence; and requests for extradition arise when a person who is accused or convicted of a criminal offence seeks refuge (or is at the time resident) in another state. Normally the alleged crime will have been committed in the state seeking extradition or aboard a ship flying its flag. Applications for extradition are made through diplomatic channels, and are reasonably straightforward where both states have agreed to specific principles in advance through the medium of an Extradition Treaty. The following principles are normally embodied in such treaties and are applied even where no treaty exists, though practice varies to a considerable extent between countries:

(a) The person whose extradition is sought must be a national of the state seeking his extradition, or a national of a third state. It is not normally the practice for a state to hand over one of its own nationals at the request of another state, though the United Kingdom and the United States of America are exceptions to this general rule.
(b) The alleged offence for which extradition is sought must be a grave one, it must normally be an offence in both states

involved, and adequate details of the individual's implication must be provided. Offences for which extradition is not normally applicable include political offences, military offences such as desertion (unless this comes within the scope of the legislation of the host state, e.g. a Visiting Forces Act), and religious offences.

The Council of Europe *European Convention on Extradition* contains the following more specific circumstances in which extradition shall *not* be applicable:

(a) if the offence in respect of which it is requested is regarded by the requested party (i.e. state) as a political offence *or as an offence connected with a political offence*;
(b) if the requested party has substantial grounds for believing that a request for extradition for an ordinary criminal offence has been made for the purpose of prosecuting or punishing a person on account of his race, religion, nationality or political opinion . . .

These provisions are qualified to the extent that the taking or attempted taking of the life of a Head of State or a member of his family shall not be deemed to be a political offence for the purposes of the Convention.

The Council of Europe *European Convention on the Suppression of Terrorism, 1977*, further stipulates, *inter alia*, that the following offences shall *not* be considered as 'political' and therefore may not be claimed as a reason for avoiding extradition:

(a) an offence within the scope of the Convention for the Suppression of Unlawful Seizure of Aircraft, signed at The Hague on 16 December 1970;
(b) an offence within the scope of the Convention for the Suppression of Unlawful Acts against the Safety of Civil Aviation, signed at Montreal on 23 September 1971;
(c) a serious offence involving an attack against the life, physical integrity or liberty of internationally protected persons, including diplomatic agents;
(d) an offence involving kidnapping, the taking of a hostage or serious unlawful detention;
(e) an offence involving the use of a bomb, grenade, rocket, automatic firearm or letter or parcel bomb if this use endangers persons;
(f) an attempt to commit any of the foregoing offences or participation as an accomplice of a person who commits or attempts to commit such an offence.

# RECOGNITION OF STATES AND GOVERNMENTS

## STATES

The question of recognition of states arises when a state undergoes a fundamental change; it may change territorially, or disappear altogether or a new state or states may emerge as a result of cession, amalgamation, federation, secession or subdivision. There are two main schools of thought in international law concerning recognition of states: one is that recognition makes the state; the other that recognition is merely the formal acceptance of an established fact. In the practice of many states recognition of a new state is essentially a political decision; but it is generally accepted that a state must have a defined territory, a permanent population and a sovereign government (which therefore has the capacity to enter into relations with other states).

## GOVERNMENTS

Governments also are capable of radical and unconstitutional change, but recognition of a new government in such circumstances is usually granted provided that it is in effective control of much the greater part of the state territory and has the obedience of the mass of the population, and that its control has a reasonable prospect of permanency.

Until recently it was the policy of the British government to make a formal announcement when it had decided to 'recognise' a new government of doubtful legitimacy, but it has now desisted from this practice mainly on the grounds that 'recognition' can be mistaken for 'approval'. Its present attitude on whether or not a new regime should be treated as a government is that it is left to be inferred from the nature of its dealings with it; and in particular whether or not it is dealing with it on a normal government-to-government basis. It nevertheless accepts the obligation to certify before the ICJ or a domestic court whether or not it recognises a particular government, if asked to do so.

*De facto* recognition of governments enables them to exercise the normal international functions of a sovereign state with reciprocal responsibilities in international law, but usually does not enable them to conclude and formally sign bilateral treaties, establish formal diplomatic relations or issue *exequaturs*: these acts are considered to imply or require recognition *de jure*. Recognition *de facto* is generally accepted as an indication that recognition *de jure* will, if all goes well, be accorded in due time. It is often used when there is an element of doubt as to the permanency of the government so recognised. In the event of civil war, the situation may arise in which a substantial part of the territory of a state is held and administered by an administration other than that of the *de jure* government. Practice, in these rare circumstances, varies between countries, but it is possible for the rebel administration to be granted *de facto* recognition in that part of the territory that it administers.

# THE EXTENT OF STATE SOVEREIGNTY AND JURISDICTION

## SOVEREIGNTY

The territorial sovereignty of a state extends over the land within the state frontier and the air space above it, but not to the upper air (outer space). In the case of maritime states, sovereignty also extends, with certain limitations, over the internal waters and the territorial sea; and the state has a measure of control over the contiguous zone, the exclusive economic zone and the continental shelf.

The international regime for determining maritime legality is based on the 1958 Geneva Convention and the 1982 Law of the Sea Convention which, though receiving a wide measure of support, has not come into force.

The major provisions of the Conventions are as follows:

Coastal states exercise sovereignty over their territorial sea up to twelve miles in extent, but foreign vessels are allowed 'innocent passage' through these waters for purposes of peaceful navigation, and permission to overfly is subject to the approval of the coastal state.

Ships and aircraft of all countries are entitled to 'transit passage' through straits used for international navigation, as long as they proceed without delay and without threatening the coastal states. States bordering the straits will be able to apply generally accepted international regulations and pollution control, but may not hamper or impede transit.

Archipelagic states, made up of a group or groups of closely related islands and interconnecting waters, have sovereignty over the sea area enclosed by straight lines drawn between the outermost points of the islands. Ships of all other states enjoy the right of passage through sea lanes designated by the archipelagic state.

Costal states have sovereign rights in a 200-nautical-mile *exclusive economic zone* with respect to natural resources and most economic activities, and are also entitled to have a certain degree of jurisdiction over scientific research and environmental preservation. All other states have freedom of navigation and overflight in the zone, as well as freedom to lay submarine cables and pipelines. When coastal states cannot fully utilise the resources available, they should provide access for other states, with a certain preference for land-locked states.

Delimitation of overlapping economic zones is to be effected by agreement on the basis of international law in order to achieve an equitable solution.

Coastal states have sovereign rights over the *continental shelf* (the national area of the sea-bed) for the purpose of exploring and exploiting it without affecting the legal status of the water or air space above. The shelf extends at least to 200 nautical miles from the shore, and up to 350 nautical miles under specified circumstances. A Commission on the Limits of the Continental Shelf will make recommendations to states on the shelf's outer boundaries. Coastal states are to share with the international community part of the revenue they derive from exploiting oil and other resources from any part of their shelf beyond 200 nautical miles. The 1982 Convention provides for delimitation of overlapping shelves in terms identical with those relating to the EEZ.

All these states enjoy the traditional freedoms of navigation, overflight, scientific research and fishing on the high seas. They have the obligation to adopt, or cooperate with other states in adopting, measures to manage and conserve living resources.

The territorial sea, the exclusive economic zone and the continental shelf of islands are to be determined in accordance with rules applicable to land territory, but rocks which cannot sustain human habitation or economic life will have no economic zone or continental shelf.

States bordering enclosed or semi-enclosed seas are expected to cooperate on the management of living resources and on environmental and research policies and activities.

Land-locked states have the right of access to and from the sea, and enjoy freedom of transit through the territory of transit states by all means of transport, subject to agreement.

A 'parallel system' provides for the exploration and exploitation of *the international sea-bed area*. All activities in the area are deemed to be under the control of the International Sea-Bed Authority, which will be authorised to conduct its own production control operations.

At the same time, the Authority will contract with private and state ventures to give them production control rights in the area, so that they can operate in parallel with the Authority. The resources of the area will be managed as a 'common heritage of mankind'. The first generation of sea-bed prospectors, known as 'pioneer operators', will have guarantees of production once production control is authorised.

States are bound to use the best practical means at their disposal to prevent and control marine pollution from any source. Coastal states, port states and flag states are responsible for preventing pollution and punishing polluters, particularly when pollution originates on board vessels. States will be liable for damage caused by violation of their international obligations to combat marine pollution. They are bound to cooperate globally and regionally in formulating rules and standards of environmental protection, and commit themselves to promoting technical assistance to developing countries in this area.

All marine scientific research in the exclusive economic zone and on the continental shelf is subject to the consent of the coastal state, but such states shall, in normal circumstances, grant consent to foreign states when the research is to be conducted for peaceful purposes as laid down in Article 246 of the Convention. A coastal state can deny permission for such research or insist on its cessation, but only under circumstances defined in the Convention. In the event of a dispute, the researching state can require the coastal states to submit the matter to international conciliation on the grounds that it is not acting in a manner compatible with the Convention.

States are bound to promote the development and *transfer of marine technology* on fair and reasonable terms and conditions. This will be done with proper regard for all legitimate interests, including the rights and duties of holders, suppliers and recipients of technology.

States are obliged to settle by peaceful means their *disputes over the interpretation or application of the Convention*. When they cannot agree on the means of settlement, they have to submit most types of disputes to compulsory procedure entailing decisions binding on all parties. They have four options: an International Tribunal for the Law of the Sea, established under the Convention: the International Court of Justice; arbitration; and special arbitration procedures. Certain types of disputes have to be submitted to conciliation, a procedure whose outcome is not binding on the parties.

## JURISDICTION

The jurisdiction of a state is generally recognised as extending over all persons, property, acts and events within its territory; and for this purpose its territory includes the Territorial Sea. However, it is customary for a state to exercise restraint in applying jurisdiction in respect of offences committed aboard foreign ships by foreign nationals, provided that the general peace is not disturbed and that the crime is not a grave one; and particularly if the consular representative of the country concerned is seen to be in control of the situation. Jurisdiction also relates to aircraft registered in, and ships flying the flag of, a state and to a state's nationals abroad, as well as universal jurisdiction over pirates and war criminals.

# NATIONALITY

The possession of a nationality grants privileges to an individual and correspondingly imposes obligations:

> 'It is for each state to determine under its own law who are its nationals. This law shall be recognised by other states in so far as it is consistent with international conventions, international custom, and the principles of law generally recognised with regard to nationality.
>
> Any question as to whether a person possesses the nationality of a particular state shall be determined in accordance with the law of that state.'

These fundamental principles set out in the Hague Convention of 1930 on the Conflict of Nationality Laws have been modified by a new principle that when a state grants nationality to a person whose association with that state is so tenuous as not to constitute a 'genuine link', other states are not bound to recognise that grant of nationality; otherwise they continue to apply.

Nationality is normally acquired by birth in the territory (*jus soli*) or as the descendant of a national (*jus sanguinis*); occasionally by naturalisation, marriage or on application, and on rare occasions as a consequence of conquest, cession or other change in the nature of a state. It is often forfeited on the acquisition of a different nationality and may be lost by renunciation, specific state legislation or, in some cases, marriage or prolonged absence. Dual nationality may occasionally result from an overlap of two countries' legislation on the subject or from exceptional circumstances. A person becomes stateless when he is deprived of his nationality and does not acquire an alternative.

The laws relating to nationality are complicated and varied, but they are very relevant to diplomats in general and to consular officers

*International law and practice*

in particular. For example, a state has the right to accord diplomatic protection to its nationals while abroad but not to others; a person usually has the right to be granted re-entry into the state of which he is a national (and therefore *prima facie* entitlement to a transit visa through an adjacent state in the direction of that state); or he may be liable to military service or subject to extradition. A duly authorised passport is generally accepted as *prima facie* evidence of nationality.

*Chapter 10*
# CONFERENCES

International negotiation is a specialised form of bargaining: when it takes the form of bilateral negotiation it may be relatively informal, but multilateral negotiation is normally conducted on a formal conference basis. As the range of international business has increased over recent years, so has *conference practice and procedure* become to a greater extent refined and standardised: that is a sort of science; and *conference diplomacy*, which is rather more an art, has, like diplomacy in all its forms, adapted to changing situations.

Conference practice and procedure are concerned with the commonly accepted rules designed to ensure the most successful possible outcome of a conference and the greatest degree of satisfaction to all participants; whereas conference diplomacy is the expertise practised by the individual delegate who seeks to gain the maximum advantage for his country. It may be said that the chairman or president of a conference requires a high degree of diplomacy to ensure a successful outcome of a conference, but as he also needs to be well acquainted with practice and procedure his skill can best be summed up in the term *conference management*.

International conferences can be classified in a number of ways. They may be:

● bilateral or multilateral;
● single-subject or multi-subject;
● *ad hoc* or regular;
● those with a permanent secretariat and those without.

International conferences may also be classified in terms of the objectives that they set out to achieve. These may be:

● to serve as a forum for the general discussion of a subject or subjects;
● to make non-binding recommendations to governments or international organisations;

- to make decisions binding on governments (in most instances *ad referendum*);
- to make decisions giving guidance or instructions to the secretariat of an inter-governmental organisation, or on the way in which a programme financed by governments should be administered, e.g. the standing or executive committees of international organisations in the interim between plenary sessions;
- to negotiate and draft a treaty or other formal international instrument;
- to provide an international exchange of information, e.g. UN Conference on the Peaceful Uses of Atomic Energy;
- to provide for the pledging of voluntary contributions to international programmes, e.g. UN High Commission for Refugees; World Food Programme.

# CONFERENCE PRACTICE AND PROCEDURE

## RULES OF PROCEDURE

The first requirement of every formal conference is a set of written rules that guide and determine the activities of the participants and to which the chairman can refer in cases of doubt or dissent. These must either be standing rules which, having been approved by a previous session, are accepted as standard procedure by subsequent sessions, e.g. the rules of procedure of the United Nations General Assembly; or they must be submitted to and approved by the conference. In the latter instance they would be circulated in draft form in advance, and would include the date and place of the meeting, adequate advance notice of which must always be given.

## THE AGENDA

The agenda of a conference lists the items of business that will be raised and the order in which each item will be considered. A draft or provisional agenda is normally prepared and circulated by the convenors or secretariat of the conference and will, in the case of regular meetings, include (i) obligatory items (e.g. the approval of the minutes of the previous meeting); (ii) items of business left over from previous session; and (iii) new submissions for consideration. The agenda must be circulated sufficiently far in advance of the conference to give participants time to study the various items of business. Similarly, items to be included on the agenda must be sent to the secretariat/convenors sufficiently early for them to be processed and the participants notified. For certain conferences (e.g. the UN General Assembly) it is obligatory for an explanatory memorandum to be circulated in respect of each substantive item on the agenda.

## COMPOSITION OF DELEGATIONS

The composition of delegations is normally provided for in the Rules of Procedure. The United Nations recognises representatives (maximum five) and alternate representatives (maximum five), and as many advisers, experts, etc., as are required.

## CREDENTIALS

Credentials are provided in a document identifying a representative and authorising him or her to act; they are usually verified by a credentials committee which reports to the plenary meeting for approval. Credentials must be issued by the proper authority and comply with the requirements of the conference rules of procedure. Full powers are required in certain instances, e.g. for adopting the text of a treaty. Paragraph 29 of the General Assembly rules of procedure allows for the provisional admission of a representative against whom objections have been raised.

## OBSERVERS

The admission and status of observers depend on the rules of procedure of the conference, but they do not in any circumstances have a vote. In the UN General Assembly it is exceptional for observers to be permitted to join in the discussions, but in the Security Council it is a common practice.

## OFFICIAL LANGUAGES AND WORKING LANGUAGES

Official languages are those in which texts and resolutions are published and in which discussions are held. Working languages are those languages used in discussion and from and into which interpretation is provided.

## PUBLICITY

Conferences can be divided into three general categories: those that are completely open and to which the public and media are invited; those that are completely closed, the public and the media being provided with a final communiqué agreed by the participants; and those that are limited to the participating members, the public and the media being informed by individual participants by means of press conferences and other forms of publicity. In practice there is a gradual spectrum of *ad hoc* arrangements between the closed and the open conference (e.g. some sessions may be open to the public and others not).

## RECORDS

A basic requirement of any conference is that there should be no doubt as to what has, and what has not, been agreed. For this purpose records of the proceedings are invariably kept and are agreed as correct by the participants. The records kept can be divided into three categories:

(a) verbatim records (manual or audio);
(b) summary records, usually prepared by the secretariat, and supervised by a *rapporteur*;
(c) the texts of resolutions only.

Participants normally have the right and opportunity to make minor alterations to improve the presentation but not the substance of a report of their intervention when it is circulated in draft form; this applies particularly in respect of verbatim reports.

## THE RIGHTS OF PARTICIPANTS

The rights of participants as well as the limitations on their activities are usually specified in the rules of procedure; and are subject always to the proviso that it is the job of the presiding officer to ensure that the conference reaches a satisfactory conclusion, and that the business of the meeting is not deliberately or needlessly obstructed. These rights are usually: the right to speak once on each question under discussion, the right to make a *point of order* (usually an objection to the remarks of a participant which are considered offensive or irrelevant); the right to make a *procedural motion* (a procedural motion relates to the conduct of the meeting and must immediately be put to the vote by the presiding officer); and the right to reply to another speaker.

## MAKING PROPOSALS AND TAKING DECISIONS

Decisions at conferences are normally taken on the basis of written proposals submitted for consideration by one or more participants: these are referred to as draft resolutions. In the UN they take the form of a preamble and an operative section; and they are normally submitted with an explanatory memorandum.

Amendments and sub-amendments to draft resolutions may be proposed (and may subsequently be withdrawn) before voting takes place. Voting is firstly on sub-amendments; secondly on 'the amendment furthest removed in substance from the original proposal' (UN General Assembly rule 92) when two or more amendments relate to the same text; and finally on the draft resolution as amended. Amendments cannot negate the substance of a resolution: they must add to, delete from or revise part of a proposal. *Explanations of vote*, i.e. a verbal statement given by a participant explaining why his vote has been cast in a particular way, are normally permitted, as are *motions for division*, which provide for separate voting on separate sections of a resolution in the event of this being specifically provided for.

## VOTING QUORUMS AND MAJORITY REQUIREMENTS

Voting is usually on the basis of a simple majority (i.e. over half) of the representatives *present and voting*; in certain instances (often for important questions) the rules of procedure may specify a two-thirds majority (i.e. two-thirds or more) of the representatives *present and voting*; or alternatively a simple or two-thirds majority of *total membership*.

Normally each country has one vote, but systems of *weighted voting* exist in, for example, the ILO and the IMF (in accordance with their rules of procedure), whereby certain categories of participants or certain countries having a greater financial or practical stake in the matter in question have more votes than others.

Rules of procedure normally provide for two specific *quorums*:

(a) the minimum number of members or participants who must be present for a vote to take place;

(b) the minimum number required to be present for business to proceed.

Voting in the Security Council is on the basis of two categories of representatives: permanent members and non-permanent members. In the General Assembly, where each country has one vote, a resolution on which there is an equally divided vote is voted on at a second meeting held within forty-eight hours, and is rejected if the votes are again equal. This procedure does not apply to the elections of officers.

Votes may be counted in various ways: by a show of hands, a roll call, by members standing or pressing a button, by secret ballot or by postal ballot.

## DETERMINING PROPOSALS BY CONSENSUS

It is unnecessary to go to the extent of casting votes on certain proposals – for example that the Conference should adjourn for lunch: the president decides that there is a consensus of opinion among the representatives that they are feeling hungry, and accordingly proposes that they should do so. This is a *consensus decision without a resolution*: it is based on an assumption by the presiding officer of what is sufficiently self-evident not to warrant taking up the time of the meeting on preparing a resolution, and is particularly applicable to procedural decisions. It is also a device that may be adopted by the presiding officer if he judges that the absence of a resolution is the best political solution to a particularly delicate situation and would be accepted as such by the participants.

A *consensus decision with a resolution* falls within the same category but is slightly more formal. It is for routine and non-controversial items, and for those items to which a minority of representatives object, but would rather not be seen to object through the publicity of a vote.

## SUBCOMMITTEES AND WORKING PARTIES

It is common practice for conferences to resolve themselves into sub-committees or working parties in order to deal with separate issues of a problem and then to consider their reports at plenary sessions. They may also provide a useful means of making recommendations on highly specialised subjects; and in cases where a conference meets at lengthy intervals are a means whereby business can be continued during the intervening periods.

## THE ELECTION OF THE OFFICIALS

The president, vice-president(s) and, where applicable, the rapporteur assume their functions either by election (as is the case in the majority of conferences) or by rotation (as the chairmanship of the Security Council). In an *ad hoc* conference the representative of the country in which the conference is being held is normally the provisional chairman.

## SEATING, PROTOCOL, ORDER OF PRECEDENCE, ETC.

In *bilateral* conferences normal diplomatic protocol is customarily observed. In *multilateral* conferences precedence is normally based on the alphabetical order of name of country (in English or French). In the UN General Assembly the point of seniority in the alphabetical order is varied for each session.

# CONFERENCE MANAGEMENT

## THE ROLE OF PRESIDING OFFICERS

There is a close parallel between the role of the presiding officer and that of the football referee. Each has the lonely and responsible task of supervising the interplay of skills and techniques between professional players each seeking to gain the maximum advantage; and within a given space of time he has to ensure that the game is played according to the rules and that the final decision is accepted by all the participants. He is provided with a book of rules (the rules of procedure) but his authority, though theoretically supreme, can have no substance unless he is able, by his sensitivity and diplomacy, to persuade those concerned that it is in their own interests to accept it and abide by his decision. Both need fairness, firmness, knowledge of the rules and very sensitive antennae; not to mention monumental patience and, at times, self-restraint.

The functions of the presiding officer fall into two categories: procedural and substantive.

### 1. Procedural functions

(a) Opening, closing and adjourning meetings.
(b) Calling on representatives to speak.

(c) Limiting the length of speeches if necessary, or if the rules so require.
(d) Giving rulings on points of order and points of procedure.
(e) Clarifying points where necessary.
(f) Calling for the termination of irrelevant remarks.
(g) Ensuring that the business of the meeting is carried out.

## 2. *Substantive functions*

(a) Carrying out *ad hoc* functions which the meeting entrusts to the presiding officer's discretion (e.g. the appointment of countries/ members to new committees).
(b) Acting as mediator, and assisting the conference to reach a conclusion. This may take the form of:

- permitting time for informal discussions;
- promoting informal discussions in which he does not participate;
- promoting informal discussions and participating in them;
- holding discussions with individual representatives to see if he can find sufficient common ground to overcome an *impasse*.

## THE SECRETARIAT

The secretariat provides the administrative backing to a conference; not only to the presiding officer and representatives during the conference, but in preparation for the conference and on its conclusion. If the secretariat is a permanent one it also continues its administrative functions between meetings, when it may assume a largely executive role, acting on the general or specific guidance of its governing body.

Before a conference, and assuming that the place of meeting has been determined, the secretariat will be mainly concerned with invitations, protocol, reception and hospitality, transport, liaison with local authorities, and the arrangement of the conference hall down to the last microphone, pencil and cup of coffee; but above all it will be concerned with the preparation and distribution of the agenda (or draft agenda) and the agenda papers, together with the rules of procedure for the conference where applicable.

While the conference is in progress the secretariat will be responsible for its entire administration, including the provision of translators and the keeping of such records of the proceedings as may be specified by the rules of procedure or required by the presiding officer. A considerable number of documents is invariably required for circulation at all stages of the proceedings – draft resolutions in particular – and shorthand typists are normally available at all reasonable hours. After the close of the conference there are two major tasks apart from the general clearing-up operations: the circulation of the Report of the Proceedings (the minutes or *procès-verbale*): these are often circulated in draft in the first instance (and nearly always so in the case of verbatim reports) so that participants may correct minor errors of punctuation, spelling or grammar (but not change the substance of their intervention); and putting into effect the various decisions that have been reached at the conference.

The head of the secretariat in many instances has certain specific functions that he is required to perform and these are usually set out in the rules of procedure. These may relate to the submission of periodic reports, the presentation of accounts, and matters relating to the staff.

# CONFERENCE DIPLOMACY

The object of conferences is to discuss problems and find solutions that are so far as possible acceptable to all participants, and this process is carried on by the traditional methods of diplomacy. However, the flourishing of multilateral diplomacy since the foundation of the United Nations has resulted in a proliferation of international organisations, conferences and committees, and has brought with it an additional dimension to traditional diplomacy: the phenomenon of group voting. Group interest does not normally override national interest, but where the national interest is not strong the group policy will be followed, mainly on the reasoning that strength lies in numbers and in unity, but also because many states with the right to vote do not have the staff to research every issue that comes before them. It is also a particularly useful system for prearranging the election of officers and generally exchanging information on matters of mutual concern.

The fundamental types of group are:

Political and cultural,
Economic development,
Regional,
Economic treaty-linked states.

Among the major groups at the present time are:

- African group
- Asian group

- The European Communities
- Group of Arab States
- Group of 77 (developing countries of Africa, Asia and Latin America, now over a 100 in number)
- Latin-American group
- Western Europe and others group.

There are in addition *ad hoc* groups which form to protect their common interests in specific matters. For example in the law of the sea conferences members of the same political or regional group opposed each other in the Continental Shelf group, the group of territorialists (200 miles territorial sea), the fishing states group or any other of the ten *ad hoc* groups that came together on this particular issue.

For a comprehensive study of conference practice and procedure, conference management and conference diplomacy see *Conference Diplomacy* by Johan Kaufmann (Leyden, Sijthoff), on which the foregoing analysis is largely based.

*Appendix A*
# ENTERTAINING

The purpose of entertaining is, of course, to afford the maximum pleasure and entertainment to one's guests. But for diplomats it has a rather more serious purpose and may in addition have the following objectives:

(a) to improve the public image of their country;
(b) to obtain opinions and information from local residents and from other diplomats;
(c) to make friends and contacts which may prove useful;
(d) to enable wives to meet and make friends with other wives so that they may share and discuss matters of mutual interest.

Also, and this is more important, it enables heads and senior members of missions informally to 'sound out' members of the Ministry of Foreign Affairs (and to a lesser extent politicians, businessmen and other diplomats) regarding proposals they would like to make, but would rather not put into writing or raise officially lest the result should be a definite, and possibly irreversible, negative.

It would be unrealistic to pretend that hard and fast rules of conduct are universally applicable, because practice varies considerably from country to country, and the range of gradations between formality and informality is great. However, it is possible to make certain generalisations, and the following deliberately err on the side of formality, on the grounds that it is safer to be too formal rather than too informal, just as it is safer for a lady to be over-dressed than under-dressed, though in both instances a telephone call to a friendly colleague is often the best way of resolving any doubts.

## OFFERING HOSPITALITY

When offering hospitality in the form of lunch or dinner, there are two tasks to be undertaken apart from organising the food and drink and making sure that the date selected does not coincide with a major national day or local religious festivity: the seating plan and invitations.

## THE SEATING PLAN

Before invitations are despatched for a lunch or dinner, a seating plan is worked out. The guests are selected, and it is essential first to ensure as far as possible that none are likely to clash (politically, personally or socially); and secondly that none are likely to object to the precedence that has been accorded to them.

The world community of states has grown with the decolonisation of the 1960s and the early 1970s, and the subsequent disintegration of the Soviet Union. Diplomatic interaction therefore is more complex, and the customs and practices of various communities need to be taken into account in diplomatic entertainment. Local custom and practice should generally prevail, with allowances being made appropriately for the sensitivities of individual guests. The essence of good diplomatic hospitality is the right atmosphere, and the compatibility of the guests is all important.

If diplomats only are present the seating plan should cause no problems, given the absolute nature of their order of precedence (attachés being a possible complication); but if non-diplomats of the host country are present the problem could easily arise, as their order of precedence is not so definite. In this latter instance senior diplomats and members of a Ministry of Foreign Affairs have a high degree of precedence, while among non-officials social status and age are major factors. In cases of doubt it is common practice to seek the advice of the Protocol Department; and it is normally found that a youthful guest will not resent giving way to age, particularly if the hostess adds a quiet word of apology.

Seating plans where only the host or the hostess is present and guests are all male or all female are based essentially on the principle that the senior guest sits on the host's right and the next senior on his left; the third senior on his right but one, the fourth senior on his left but one, and so on (in Nordic countries, contrary to normal practice, seniority is on the left). The following examples may be adapted to circular tables without basic change:

*All male/female seating plan: host/hostess and seven guests*

If a host were holding a luncheon or dinner in honour of a specific guest he might adopt the following plan:

When both host and hostess are present the principle is extended as follows:

*Mixed seating plan: host, hostess and six couples (men underlined)*

The same rules apply when the host and hostess sit opposite each other in the centre of the long sides of the table. This arrangement has many advantages, but tends to leave those at the ends of the table rather out in the cold: a situation aggravated if, as sometimes happens, the end places are not filled.

The hostess normally sits facing the door leading to the kitchen, so that she may more effectively control her staff.

It is not the practice in European countries for wives to be placed next to their husbands, nor do two ladies or two gentlemen normally sit next to each other, but in this respect the custom of the country should be adhered to. It will be found that tables of 6, 10 and 14 work out satisfactorily if the host and hostess are at opposite ends of a rectangular table, whereas 8 and 12 do not permit host and hostess to sit at opposite ends. However 14 is risky, because if one person drops out the hostess is left with – to some – an unlucky 13.

It may sometimes happen that a couple drop out, or that one of the partners is unable to attend at the last minute. In these instances members of one's own mission or friendly colleagues may be asked to help out. When members of an ambassador's or a high commissioner's staff include their head of mission and his wife in the guest list for a lunch or dinner it is customary for the latter to be seated as though they were the hosts in the same way as a Foreign Minister or a Head of States does when visiting one of his own missions.

## INVITATIONS

These should be sent out two or three weeks before the event: shorter notice might not give the hosts time to invite an alternative guest if it is refused, and longer notice might embarrass a guest who, for some reason, might wish to refuse on some fictitious grounds, e.g. that he had a prior engagement.

Invitations are written in the third person and normally in the following style:

> *The Ambassador of ............................... and Mrs 'X'*
> *Request the pleasure of the company*
> *of*
> *Mr and Mrs 'Y'*
> *at Lunch*
> *on Thursday 17 September at 1.15 p.m.*

Address                                                    R.S.V.P.

In certain instances (e.g. if inviting the Minister for Foreign Affairs) one would request 'the *honour* of the company'. An alternative method (the current practice for the particular post should always be followed) is to issue the invitation by telephone, if appropriate through secretaries. If the answer is in the affirmative, the host or hostess then sends an invitation card with the necessary details and with the initials 'p.m.' or the words 'to remind', and encloses a list of guests giving their titles and function. This ensures that all those invited know in advance who the other guests are and what they do – an obvious aid to successful entertaining.

An invitation to dinner would include the type of dress: e.g. 'Black Tie' or Lounge suit or for ladies 'Long dress' where appropriate.

## A DINNER PARTY

It is customary at a gathering of ten or more for a table plan to be displayed so that guests may know their table places in advance; otherwise it is the task of the hostess to indicate to guests where they sit when they enter the dining-room. When ten or more are invited all places should have name cards.

If the time of the dinner is stated as 7.30 for 8 p.m. it is expected that guests will arrive soon after 7.30 p.m. (never before); they will be introduced to the other guests and will drink fruit juice or aperitifs until about 8 p.m. (or later if any of the guests have been late in arriving), after which time dinner will be served.

Guests will be welcomed by the host and hostess and introduced to the other guests present. If guests arrive late and the host and hostess are not awaiting them on their entry into the room, they must seek them out, apologising for their lateness, whereupon they will be introduced to those already present.

As soon as guests have been received and introduced, they will be offered a drink. The following are usually served as aperitifs:

Sherry, dry
White wine
Gin and tonic water, with preferably a slice of lemon peel (the 'zest')
Whisky (Scotch) and soda; alternatively Bourbon Fruit juice

When all the members of the party are assembled and when the hostess has been told by a member of the staff that dinner is ready, she will lead the guests into the dining-room. On very formal occasions the gentlemen will be asked to escort specific ladies to their places, but such a procedure is rare. It is, however, a courtesy to help the lady on one's right to seat herself at the table by pulling out her chair for her. (It is also a nice introduction).

The choice of menu will depend on personal taste and circumstances, but dietary restrictions of guests on account of health or religion have always to be taken into account.

During the meal it is the duty of the host and hostess – and indeed of all the guests – to ensure that no individual or group monopolises the conversation to the exclusion of any one of the company. The men, in particular, should engage the ladies on either side of them in conversation, irrespective of their charm or vivacity, to an equal extent throughout the meal.

At the end of the meal, when all have finished, the hostess catches the eye of the senior lady present to ensure that she is ready to leave the table, and will then rise from her seat; that being a signal for all to rise. If it is the practice for the men to remain at the table to discuss matters of business after the ladies have left they will normally congregate at one end for their coffee, cigars and liqueurs. If lady diplomats are present, and wish to join in the discussions, it is the responsibility of the host to ensure that they feel welcome to do so. It is not advisable to smoke during a meal, as this may cause offence to others; nor should cigars be lit until after the toast has been given or the port has been circulated (customarily clockwise). In order to bring the evening to a close drinks may be served around 10.30 p.m. (the time depending on local custom), after which the senior guest will leave followed by the others. If an Ambassador is present as a guest and also a member of his staff, the latter should not leave before his head of mission. Ambassadors and other particularly important guests are normally escorted to their cars.

After an interval of two or three days it is customary in some countries for guests to send a visiting card marked 'p.r. (*pour remercier*), to say 'thank you' for the dinner or, more personally, to write a 'thank-you' letter.

## A BUFFET DINNER

In recent times a popular method of entertaining has been the Buffet Dinner. It provides an opportunity to offer a variety of dishes to meet various tastes and dietary restrictions, and it enables the host and hostess more effectively to move among their guests. There are many variations. Guests may be formally seated at round tables of six or eight where the first course is served, with guests subsequently helping themselves at the Buffet Table. In rather formal Buffet Dinners it would not be unusual for the second course to be served, and also the dessert. A slightly less formal buffet would be to arrange table placings by name at round or card tables, but no courses would be served: guests would help themselves. An informal Buffet Dinner would be one without place settings, but with round tables or card tables for guests to sit where they will. And finally a Buffet Dinner organised by a diplomat in a small house or apartment could be quite informal with guests sitting wherever seats are available or even standing.

## A LUNCH PARTY

The invitation, seating plan and other arrangements (including the leaving of cards, p.r.) are the same as for a dinner, but the meal will be lighter and the general atmosphere of the party is likely to be less formal. Ladies (guests) may or may not wear hats, according to the custom of the country (the hostess never wears a hat). Guests are normally invited at 1 o'clock for 1.15 p.m., in which case they would leave between 2.15 and 2.30 p.m. They will be offered aperitifs or fruit juice on arrival and, after the meal, coffee and liqueurs.

## A COFFEE PARTY (*LADIES*)

Coffee parties are a useful, simple and fairly informal method of enabling wives to meet other wives; but they are not popular with late risers. It may or may not be the custom to wear hats; cards 'p.r.' are not left. If invited for 11 o'clock, guests would leave soon after 12 noon.

## A TEA PARTY (*LADIES*)

Tea parties tend to be rather formal, and last approximately from 4 o'clock until 5.15 p.m. It may or may not be the custom to wear hats; card are not left.

## A VIN D'HONNEUR

When there is a specific cause for celebration or for honouring an individual or a group of people – for example when a Head of Mission has presented his credentials, an agreement has been signed or a delegation has arrived – a Vin d'Honneur is commonly offered. Drinks, both alcoholic and non-alcoholic – often champagne – are served, and the occasion, which is quite formal, usually lasts for about an hour.

155

## GENERAL OBSERVATIONS

For Muslims and people of the Judaic faith, pork or pork products are taboo, and orthodox Muslims and Jews will not eat other meats unless they are halal or kosher respectively. In a non-Muslim state or one where there is not a large Jewish population, obtaining such foods may be problematic. It would therefore not be unreasonable to serve non-halal or non-kosher meats to Muslim or Jewish guests but it would be improper to serve pork or pork products. If one has guests of the Hindu faith, it would be improper to serve beef, but it would not be unreasonable to serve a vegetarian meal, making particular provision for one's vegetarian guests. It would therefore be a thoughtful gesture to enquire about any dietary restrictions your guests may have when inviting them to a function, making appropriate arrangements to meet particular sensitivities.

In East Asia, the preferred implements for eating are chopsticks. In Southeast and South Asia and in West Asia one uses one's fingers, but it is taboo to use the left hand. In an East Asian Embassy in a Western capital or in an East Asian post it is not uncommon for guests to be provided with chopsticks, and in other Asian and African posts there may be occasions when one would be expected to use one's fingers. When in doubt the rule is to do as one's host or hostess does.

In many non-European societies it is considered impolite to hand or receive anything with the left hand. Also in some societies it is impolite to point with the index finger or to sit in a manner where the soles of your feet or shoes are visible to your host or guests. In many Asian societies it is customary to remove one's shoes before entering a home. Moreover, more orthodox Muslims do not shake the hand of a person of the opposite sex. In all such situations it would be wise to be guided by local custom and practice. It is also useful to bear in mind that smoking is actively discouraged by some hosts and hostesses. Smokers should look out for signs: the non-availability of ashtrays being a clear signal that smoking is not welcome.

# ACCEPTING HOSPITALITY

Invitations in writing should be answered promptly, preferably within twenty-four hours. If they are not answered promptly and the answer is in the negative, the hostess will not have an opportunity to find a suitable substitute. The reply is in the third person, and on the following lines:

Mr and Mrs X thank Mr and Mrs Y for their kind
invitation to dinner on Thursday 3rd May at
7.30 p.m. and have much pleasure in accepting.

*or*

Mr and Mrs X thank Mr and Mrs Y for their kind
invitation to dinner on Thursday 3rd May at
7.30 p.m. but very much regret that they will be
unable to accept as they will be away from .....................
on that date (or 'owing to a previous engagement').

If a husband and wife are invited to lunch or dinner and only one
can attend, it is usual to decline on behalf of both. If, however, a
verbal understanding is reached, or if the occasion does not involve
a seating arrangement (e.g. a reception), then the one may accept for
himself (very rarely herself) alone, the reply being on the following
lines:

Mr and Mrs X thank Mr and Mrs Y for their kind
invitation to a reception on Thursday 3rd May at 9
p.m. Mrs X very much regrets that she will be
unable to attend, but Mr X has much pleasure in
accepting.

The time of a function is specified on the invitation; for lunch or
dinner it is considered a politeness to arrive at the time stated,
or preferably five minutes later. For most receptions and cocktail
parties the time of arrival is more flexible, as it must be if two or
more have to be attended on the same night. In these circumstances
it is not unknown for husband and wife to fulfil an engagement
separately, usually meeting at the final function; and in the case of
representation at national day celebrations, members of a mission
will often take it in turn to be present. If however, the reception is
given for an occasion when a speech is likely to be made, for example
the award of a decoration or a farewell, then it is important to arrive
within 15–20 minutes of the time stated on the invitation.

The time of departure from a function varies, but it is better to
be brief than to overstay one's welcome.


## SAYING 'THANK YOU'

The counterpart to generous hospitality by the host or hostess is
appreciation on the part of the guest, and ways of showing this
will depend both on the occasion and the custom of the country.

157

*Entertaining*

After a mixed dinner, a mark of appreciation would normally be appropriate, and this might take the form of flowers to the hostess either before or after the occasion, or for those of less exuberant temperament the humble 'thank-you letter'. This follows the simple rule that it should contain only sentiments of appreciation, and might be on the following lines:

> Dear Mrs ....................
>
> I am writing to say how very much my husband and I appreciated your kind hospitality last night.
>
> The dinner was a most enjoyable occasion, and we are very grateful for your kind invitation.
>
> Yours sincerely,

## INTRODUCING PEOPLE

A gentleman is normally presented or introduced to a lady; and a junior is always presented to a senior, e.g.

> 'Mrs Smith, may I introduce Mr Jones.'

Similarly:

> 'Your Excellency (Ambassador), may I present Mr Robbins, Counsellor in the Ruritanian Embassy.

When introducing two people, the simple presentation of the one to the other by name is rarely adequate. If, as at a cocktail party, they may be expected to embark on a conversation it is essential to give a brief description of their respective functions, e.g. 'Mrs Smith, may I introduce Mr Silva? Mr Silva is Cultural Attaché at the Brasilian Embassy and knows Scandinavia well. Mrs Smith's husband is a director of Wotherspoons, and they have just arrived from Oslo.'

## VISITING CARDS

The visiting card is a useful device in that it performs functions on behalf of its owner. It may be delivered personally, delivered by chauffeur or sent by post, according to local custom and the degree of intimacy that it is designed to convey. For example, if the Ruritanian Counsellor, who is married, arrives at a post he may (if it is the local practice) send or take to Counsellors of other missions (who are married) two of his own cards and one of his wife's; and the two parties would consider themselves as being formally introduced to each other and free to act accordingly. The reason for the Ruritanian Counsellor presenting two of his own cards and one of his wife's is that he may present his compliments to another Counsellor and to that Counsellor's wife; but a lady in these circumstances will only present her compliments to another lady: it would not be correct for her to present them to a man. To those who are unmarried he would send or take one card of his own.

Visiting cards may also convey specific messages, which take the form of initials pencilled at the bottom. The most common ones are:

p.p     *pour présentation*: to introduce or present somebody
p.p.c.  *pour prendre congé*: to take one's leave, or say farewell
p.r.    *pour remercier*: to thank, e.g. for a dinner
p.c.    *pour condoléances*: to express condolences
p.m.   *pour mémoire*: to remind.

Visiting cards may be 'cornered' (i.e. the top lefthand corner is folded down, then back nearly to its original place) to indicate that they have been presented personally.

It is usual for a married diplomat to have at least two sets of cards: one with his name, rank and embassy; and one bearing only his name and that of his wife.

Perhaps the most important function of a visiting card is to serve as a reminder of new acquaintances made at receptions and other functions – their name, initials, address and rank. Diplomats on all such occasions should go well equipped with a supply of their own cards for distribution, and in their turn can build up a valuable collection of other people's as a source of reference.

# WINES, COCKTAILS AND LIQUEURS

## WINES

Wines are part of the tradition of diplomacy in many countries, and although the past decade has witnessed the transformation of wine-production from the age-old skill of viticulture to its modern status as a branch of the agro-chemical industry, a basic knowledge of the subject is not entirely irrelevant.

*(a) Table wines*, i.e. those drunk with a meal, may he categorised in various ways, e.g. by colour – red, rosé (pink) or white; by taste – sweet, medium or dry; by effervescence – sparkling or still; by 'body'

– full-bodied or light (thin), and, of course, by country. The 'vintage' of a wine is the year in which the grapes were harvested. Some years have produced better wines than others, and a 'vintage chart' providing the relevant information can be purchased for a small sum; if a wine is 'non-vintage' it may be a blend of wines of various years.

French and German tables wines have perhaps the greatest international appeal, and the most popular are:

*French*
Red:   Bordeaux
       Burgundy
       Rhône
White: Champagne (non-vintage is usually lighter than vintage)
       Bourdeaux (mostly medium/dry) but:
           Barsac (sweet)
           Sauterne (sweet)
       Burgundy (fairly dry; slightly flinty flavour)

*German*
White: Mosel (dry and fresh)
       Rhine wines: (often called *hock*)
           Rheinhessen
           Rheinpfalz
           Rheingau
           Nahe

*(b) Fortified wines* are wines to which alcohol (usually brandy) has been added. They may be drunk before a meal as aperitifs, or at the end of a meal as dessert wines.

At the end of a meal port wine is a traditional drink in many countries. Vintage port is matured mainly in the bottle; tawny (and ruby) are matured in the wood and should not be kept long in the bottle. A suitable alternative is madeira: Bual, Malvasia (Malmsey) or Verdelho.

Vintage ports and some red wines develop with age a deposit at the bottom of the bottle and need decanting; the clear wine is poured carefully into another vessel (usually a 'decanter') and the dregs or lees are left behind.

*(c) Spiced and fortified wines* include vermouths: red (sweet) and white (dry); and a variety to be found under trade names such as Cinzano, Dubonnet, etc.

*Choosing wines*
The choice of wines with a meal is essentially a matter for individual taste, but as a general rule dry white wine goes with fish; red wine

with meat, and sweet wine with sweets. The following may be taken as an example, but much depends on whether the food is plainly or richly prepared.

| | |
|---|---|
| Soup | Dry sherry or madeira |
| Fish | Plainly cooked: Moselle; in rich sauce: white Burgundy. |
| White meat | Plainly cooked – Rhine spätlese; in a rich sauce – red burgundy |
| Roast or game | Claret, red burgundy, red Rioja Gran Reserva |
| Sweets | Sauterne or sweet hock |
| Cheese | Red wine, Port |
| Dessert | Port or madeira |

Red wines are best if served at room temperature (in cold climates they are usually served too cold). They should not be rapidly heated (e.g. placed in hot water or too close to a fire); and if possible they should be brought into the dining-room several hours before the meal and allowed to 'rest', and the heavier ones given time to 'breathe' with the cork extracted, care being taken that they are not jostled. All white wines should be served chilled; sweet white wines may be served cold.

## COCKTAILS

Cocktails are mixtures of drinks, often of unknown content and potency, which is a good *prima facie* reason for avoiding them. Some, nevertheless, are eminently respectable and widely drunk, the most popular being:

Dry Martini: gin and dry (usually French) vermouth
Sweet Martini: gin and sweet (usually Italian) vermouth
Champagne cocktail: champagne and, e.g. Cognac and bitters.

A cocktail (or other drink) 'on the rocks' is one which is poured over chipped ice in the glass.

## LIQUEURS

Liqueurs are potent, concentrated drinks and are taken after a meal. Mostly they have a brandy base to which herbs, fruit and/or syrup are added.

*Entertaining*

# CATEGORIES OF WINES

The laws relating to German and French wines (the only ones dealt with here for reasons of brevity, though Spanish, Italian, Swiss, Austrian, North American, Chilean and Australian wines are often excellent) have been clarified so that the label will now provide a reasonable description of what the bottle is likely to contain; and are as follows.

## FRENCH WINES

There are three categories of French table wines: firstly, *'Appellation Controlée'* (A.C.) which will include the fine wines; secondly, *'Vin Délimité de Qualité Supérieur'* (V.D.Q.S.) and finally, *'Vin de Table'* (Vin de Pays); the two latter being mainly for local consumption.

*Bordeaux: The red A.C. wines* (claret) will bear the year of the vintage and the name of one of its regions, e.g. Haut Médoc (or alternatively one of its most famous communes St-Estèphe, Pauillac, St-Julien or Margaux), Graves, St-Emilion, Pomerol.

*The white A.C. wines* which are famous are sweet: from Sauternes, which includes the villages of Barsac, and the outstanding Château Yquem.

The higher quality red and white Bordeaux wines are usually bottled on the Estate and will bear on the label the words 'mis en bouteilles dans nos caves', 'chais' or 'celliers'; whilst the cork will be marked 'mis en bouteille' . . . etc. The length of the cork usually indicates the quality of the wine: the longer, the better.

Certain wines from Bordeaux in the Appellation Controllée category are entitled to be described as *'classed growths'* on the basis of classification awards, and may add to their label 'premier cru', 'deuxième cru', etc., to 'cinquième cru' depending on their value in 1855 when the awards were made. Some of lesser standing may be styled 'Cru Bourgeois' or 'Cru Artisan'; and the label of an A.C. wine will invariably carry the year of the vintage.

As a general rule fine wines from Bordeaux (and from the Loire) will bear the name of a Château (i.e. the vineyard).

*Burgundy*: Burgundy may come under varous general headings such as 'Bourgogne', 'Côte de Beaune Villages', etc., but the really fine wines are from the *Côte de Nuits* (preferably red), e.g. Fixin, Gevrey Chambertin; and from the *Côte de Beaune* (preferably white), e.g. Volnay, Meursault.

Wines from Burgundy do not bear the name of a Château, but may show the name of the 'Clos', 'Domaine' or occasionally the vineyard where appropriate; and the white wines are all dry. Further south in the Burgundy region come *Macon* (red and white); and *Beaujolais* which is almost entirely red. Beaujolais *primeur* is drunk within a few months of the vintage.

The *Côtes du Rhône* produces some good, often slightly sharp-tasting full-bodied red wine especially from Châteauneuf-du-Pape.

The *Loire Valley* produces a wide variety of red, rosé and white wines, bearing famous names such as Sancerre and Muscadet.

Wines from *Alsace* are mainly light, clean and dry; and *Champagne* needs no introduction.

GERMAN WINES

Production of German wine falls into three categories: (1) Table wine, (2) Quality wine and (3) specially graded Quality wines.

1. *Tafelwein*: light, pleasant wines consumed mainly in Germany.
2. *Qualitätswein*: quality wine with more body, made from approved grape varieties. Within this category falls *Liebfraumilch*, which is a Qualitätswein from Rheinpfalz, Rheinhessen, Nahe or Rheingau.
3. *Qualitätswein mit prädikat*: the highest category of German wine. These quality wines which are specially graded must be from approved grape varieties.
   *Kabinett*: lightest of these wines, usually dry, elegant and delicate.
   *Spätlese*: literally means late harvest; wines have more body, and a degree of sweetness.
   *Auslese*: rich wines made from the ripest bunches of grapes, picked individually.
   *Beerenauslese*: wines of exceptional quality, from individually selected grapes; sweet and full-bodied.
   *Trockenbeerenauslese*: highest category of German viticulture; a wine rarely made; from individually selected grapes, shrivelled almost to raisins.
   *Eiswein*: rare wine made from grapes harvested and crushed while still frozen.
   *Sekt*: sparkling wine, whose effervescence reflects characteristics of the Rhine and Mosel.

The label will normally also include the name of the vineyard/property (e.g. the Weingut) and the region (the Bereich); the official growers' number (the Amtliche Prüfungsnummer); the type of grape (e.g. Riesling, Müller-Thurgau, Sylvaner); and the word Erzeuger-Abfüllung if the wine is estate bottled.

# NON-ALCOHOLIC DRINKS

It should always be borne in mind that many people, for a variety of reasons, drink non-alcoholic beverages, and that as much care should be taken in providing for their taste as is taken for those preferring alcohol.

*Appendix B*

# INTERNATIONAL ABBREVIATIONS

The letters 'q.v.' indicate that the subject is referred to elsewhere in the text.

| | |
|---|---|
| ACP | African, Caribbean and Pacific Countries, European Community/Lomé Convention; also group of states with observer status in the General Assembly |
| AID | Agency for International Development (US Government Agency) |
| ALADI | Latin American Integration Association (q.v.) |
| ANZUS | Australia, New Zealand and USA Treaty Organisation |
| ASAT | Anti-satellite systems |
| ASEAN | Association of Southeast Asian Nations (q.v.) |
| BENELUX | Customs Union of Belgium, the Netherlands and Luxembourg |
| BIS | Bank for International Settlements (q.v.) |
| B-ISDN | Broadband integrated services digital network |
| CABEI | Central American Bank for Economic Integration |
| CARICOM | The Caribbean Community (q.v.) |
| CBM | Confidence building measures |
| CCCN | Customs Cooperation Council Nomenclature |
| CDC | Commonwealth Development Corporation (UK Government Agency) |
| CEAO | Economic Community of West Africa (q.v.) |
| CEEAC | Economic Community of Central African States |
| CERN | European Council for Nuclear Research |
| CFC | Chlorofluorocarbon |
| CGCED | Caribbean Group for Cooperation in Economic Development |

| | |
|---|---|
| CIAP | Inter-American Committee on the Alliance for Progress |
| CIPEC | Intergovernmental Committee of Copper-Exporting Countries |
| CNUCED | See UNCTAD |
| COCOM | Coordinating Committee for Multilateral Export Controls |
| CODESA | Conference on democracy in South Africa |
| CONDECA | Central American Defence Council |
| COREPER | Council of Permanent Representatives (European Community) (q.v.) |
| CPE | Centrally Planned Economy |
| CPISA | Convention on the privileges and immunities of Specialised Agencies |
| CPIUN | Convention on the privileges and immunities of the UN |
| CRSIO | Convention on the representation of states in their relations with international organisations |
| CSM | Convention on Special Missions |
| CSCE | Conference on Security and Cooperation in Europe |
| DAC | Development Assistance Committee (OECD) |
| DCM | Deputy Chief of Mission |
| EAEC | European Atomic Energy Community (Euratom) |
| EBRD | European Bank for Reconstruction and Development |
| EC | European Community |
| ECA | Economic Commission for Africa (UN) |
| ECE | Economic Commission for Europe (UN) |
| ECLAC | Economic Commission for Latin America and the Caribbean (UN) |
| ECOSOC | Economic and Social Council (UN) |
| ECOWAS | Economic Community of West African States (q.v.) |
| ECSC | European Coal and Steel Community |
| ECU | European Currency Unit (q.v.) |
| EDF | European Development Fund (EC) |
| EDTV | Enhanced definition television |
| EEA | European Economic Area |
| EEZ | Exclusive Economic Zone (q.v.) |
| EFTA | European Free Trade Association (q.v.) |
| EIB | European Investment Bank (EEC) |

| | |
|---|---|
| ELDO | European Launcher Development Organisation (EC) |
| EMI | European Monetary Institute (EC) |
| EMS | European Monetary System |
| EMU | Economic and monetary union (EC) |
| ENEA | European Nuclear Energy Agency (OECD) |
| EPC | European Political Cooperation (q.v.) |
| ERM | European Exchange Rate Mechanism (EC) |
| ESCAP | Economic and Social Commission for Asia and the Pacific (UN) |
| ESRO | European Space Research Organisation |
| EURATOM | European Atomic Energy Community (q.v.) |
| FAO | Food and Agriculture Organisation (q.v.) |
| FCO | Foreign and Commonwealth Office (UK) |
| GAB | General agreement to borrow (IBRD) |
| GATT | General Agreement on Tariffs and Trade (q.v.) |
| GDP | Gross Domestic Product (q.v.) |
| GEF | Global environment facility (IBRD) |
| GNP | Gross National Product (q.v.) |
| GSP | Generalised System of Preferences (q.v.) |
| HABITAT | United Nations Centre for Human Settlements (Nairobi) |
| HDTV | High definition television |
| IADB | Inter-American Development Bank |
| IAEA | International Atomic Energy Agency (q.v.) |
| IATA | International Air Transport Association |
| IBRD | International Bank for Reconstruction and Development (q.v.) |
| ICAO | International Civil Aviation Organisation (q.v.) |
| ICBM | Inter-Continental Ballistic Missile |
| ICFTU | International Confederation of Free Trade Unions (Brussels) |
| ICJ | International Court of Justice (q.v.) |
| ICO | Islamic Conference Organisation (q.v.) |
| IDA | International Development Association (IBRD) (q.v.) |
| IDB | Inter-American Development Bank |
| IFAD | International Fund for Agricultural Development (q.v.) |
| IFC | International Finance Corporation (IBRD) (q.v.) |
| ILC | International Law Commission (q.v.) |

| | |
|---|---|
| ILO | International Labour Organisation (q.v.) |
| IMF | International Monetary Fund (q.v.) |
| IMO | International Maritime Organisation (q.v.) |
| INF | Intermediate Nuclear Forces |
| INIS | International Nuclear Information System |
| INSTRAW | International Research and Training Institute for the Advancement of Women (q.v.) |
| INTERPOL | International Criminal Police Organisation |
| ITU | International Telecommunications Union (q.v.) |
| | |
| LAIA | Latin American Integration Association (q.v.) |
| LDC | Less Developed Country |
| LLDC | Least Developed Country |
| | |
| MBFR | Mutual and Balanced Force Reductions |
| MCCA | Central American Common Market (q.v.) |
| MERCOSUR | Southern cone common market (q.v.) |
| MFA | Multi-fibre Arrangement |
| MFN | Most-favoured Nation |
| MIGA | Multilateral Investment Guarantee Agency (IBRD) |
| MIRV | Multiple independently targetable re-entry vehicle |
| | |
| NAFTA | North American Free Trade Agreement (q.v.) |
| NATO | North Atlantic Treaty Organisation (q.v.) |
| NDI | National Disposable Income (takes account of the terms of trade, q.v.) |
| NGO | Non-governmental Organisation |
| NIC | Newly Industrialising Country |
| NIEO | New International Economic Order |
| NORDEK | Nordic Union |
| NPT | Treaty on the Non-Proliferation of Nuclear Weapons |
| | |
| OAPEC | Organisation of Arab Petroleum Exporting Countries |
| OAS | Organisation of American States (q.v.) |
| OAU | Organisation of African Unity (q.v.) |
| OCAS | Organisation of Central American States |
| ODA | Official Development Assistance (UNCTAD) |
| ODA | Overseas Development Administration (UK) |
| ODECA | Organisation of Central American States |
| ODIHR | Office for Democratic Institutions and Human Rights (CSCE) |

| | |
|---|---|
| OEA | Organisation of American States (q.v.) |
| OECD | Organisation for Economic Cooperation and Development (q.v.) |
| OECS | Organisation of Eastern Caribbean States (q.v.) |
| OPEC | Organisation of the Petroleum Exporting Countries (q.v.) |
| | |
| p.a. | per annum: yearly |
| PALOP | Organisation of Lusophone African States |
| p.c. | per capita: per person |
| PLO | Palestine Liberation Organisation |
| PPP | Purchasing power parity |
| | |
| q.v. | Quod vide: the immediately preceding word or phrase appears elsewhere in the text |
| | |
| R and D | Research and Development |
| RDCD | Regional Cooperation Among Developing Countries |
| RDF | Rapid Deployment Force |
| | |
| SAARC | South Asian Association for Regional Cooperation (q.v.) |
| SADC | Southern African Development Community (q.v.) |
| SALS | Structured adjustment loans (IBRD, q.v.) |
| SALT | Strategic Arms Limitation Talks |
| SAM | Surface-to-air Missile |
| SATCOM | Satellite Communication |
| SDI | Strategic Defence Initiative |
| SDR | Special drawing rights (IMF) (q.v.) |
| SECALS | Sector adjustment loans (IBRD, q.v.) |
| SELA | Latin American Economic System (q.v.) |
| SPC | South Pacific Commission (q.v.) |
| SPEC | South Pacific Bureau for Economic Cooperation (q.v.) |
| SPF | South Pacific Forum (q.v.) |
| SRO | Single Regional Organisation (q.v.) |
| STABEX | System of Stabilisation of Export Earnings (Lomé Convention) (q.v.) |
| START | Strategic Arms Reduction Talks ('SALT 3') |
| SYSMIN | System of Stabilisation of Mining Exports (Lomé Convention) |
| | |
| TNC | Transnational Corporation |

| | |
|---|---|
| UAM | Union Africaine et Malagache |
| UDEAC | Central African Customs and Economic Union |
| UEAC | Union of Central African States (q.v.) |
| UNCDF | United Nations Capital Development Fund |
| UNCITRAL | UN Commission on International Trade Law |
| UNCTAD | United Nations Conference on Trade and Development (q.v.) |
| UNDC | UN Disarmanent Commission (q.v.) |
| UNDOF | UN Disengagement Observer Force |
| UNDP | United Nations Development Programme (q.v.) |
| UNDRO | United Nations Disaster Relief Office |
| UNEP | United Nations Environment Programme (q.v.) |
| UNESCO | United Nations Educational Scientific and Cultural Organisation (q.v.) |
| UNFICYP | United Nations Peace-keeping Force in Cyprus |
| UNFPA | United Nations Fund for Population Activities (q.v.) |
| UNHCR | United Nations High Commissioner for Refugees (q.v.) |
| UNICEF | United Nations Childrens Fund (q.v.) |
| UNIDO | United Nations Industrial Development Organisation (q.v.) |
| UNIFIL | United Nations Interim Force in Lebanon |
| UNITAR | United Nations Institute for Training and Research (q.v.) |
| UNRISD | United Nations Research Institute for Social Development |
| UNRWA | United Nations Relief and Works Agency for Palestine Refugees in the Near East (q.v.) |
| UNSSD | UN Special Session on Disarmament (q.v.) |
| UNTSO | United Nations Truce Supervision Organisation |
| UNU | United Nations University |
| UPU | Universal Postal Union (q.v.) |
| | |
| VER | Voluntary Export Restriction (EC) |
| VRA | Voluntary Restraint Arrangement (GATT) |
| | |
| WEU | Western European Union (q.v.) |
| WFC | World Food Council |
| WFP | World Food Programme (UN/FAO, q.v.) |
| WHO | World Health Organisation (q.v.) |
| WIPO | World Intellectual Property Organisation (q.v.) |
| WMO | World Meteorological Organisation (q.v.) |

# ISLAMIC FESTIVALS

The two major festivals in the Islamic calendar, apart from the Prophet's birthday, the Ascension of the Prophet and the Islamic and Christian New Years, are: (a) the *īd al fitr* or Little Festival which marks the end of the month *Ramadān* and is held during the first days of the following month. *Shawwāl*; and (b) the *ıd al adha al mubārak* or Great Festival which lasts for four days and is associated with the sacrifice at Minā made by the pilgrims who are undertaking the *Hajj* to Mecca.

During the entire month of *Ramadān* fasting takes place from dawn to sunset, and a special festival is the Day of Decrees on the twenty-seventh of the month.

The Islamic calendar takes as its starting point the Prophet's move from Mecca to Medina (the *Hijra*) on 16 July AD 622 (or 'CE' for Christian era) which became the first day of the Islamic era ('AH' for *Anno Hegirae*). The calendar is based on the lunar month of 29½ days with twelve months in the year (the months consisting of twenty-nine and thirty days alternately) which results in a year of 354 days. The Islamic year is consequently shorter by approximately eleven days than the solar year, and *Ramadān* and other festivals are therefore eleven days earlier each year according to the non-Islamic (or Gregorian) calendar. It should be noted that, traditionally, a 'day' starts at sunset. Friday is the Day of Prayer when all offices are closed; and in some countries the Thursday is included in this 'week-end'.

In addition, Shī'ite Muslims celebrate the death at Kerbela of Husain, grandson of the Prophet and son of Alī the fourth Caliph. This festival begins on the first day of Muharram (the first month of the Islamic year) and comes to a climax on the tenth day, the anniversary of Husain's death in the year 61 AH (10 October AD 680). The occasion is one of deep mourning.

*Appendix D*

# THE ENVIRONMENT

The protection of the local environment has long been a matter of national concern, to be dealt with by politicians (such as the UK Clean Air Act of 1956), and of regional concern to be dealt with by diplomats, negotiating such treaties as the Rhine River Treaty and the 1991 Protocol for the Protection of the Environment in the Antarctic.

Now, as a result of man's ability to influence the world's climate through rapid advances in technology and a dramatic increase in population, it has become a matter of major international concern, of urgency and priority for diplomats. Population pressures, industrialisation, new technologies, a build-up of carbon dioxide ($CO_2$) and other 'greenhouse' gases in the atmosphere, new pollutants, enhanced material expectations, changes in methods of farming the land and sea – all have combined to threaten the stability of the world's climatic system, and with it the world's existing ecosystem. It is difficult to gauge the extent of this threat to the world's climate, since change is the essence of climate as a consequence of global and universal factors outside man's knowledge and influence – such as the change in the earth's angle on its axis or the phases of sunspots, and little is known of the interrelationships between these factors. Accurate measurements have been available for decades, whereas climatic changes are to be reckoned in millennia; nevertheless the protection of the global environment is a supreme example of the need for positive diplomacy and international cooperation; whilst the destructive effect of present practices on the ecosystem – such as desertification and loss of bio-diversity – are plain for all to see. Environmental damage such as acid rain, toxic waste and marine pollution are being actively tackled, but there are four major areas of global concern, which can only be resolved by positive diplomacy on a comprehensive international basis:

# (1)  THE OZONE LAYER

A major factor in maintaining the world's existing ecohabitat is a concentrated layer of ozone gas approximately fifteen miles above the earth's surface. This acts as a shield preventing a harmful quantity of the sun's ultra-violet rays from reaching the earth. It is only in recent years that appropriate technology has enabled the ozone layer to be measured, but during this time it has become evident that it is decreasing steadily and substantially. It is also known that chlorofluorocarbon gases (CFCs) destroy ozone molecules. These are being produced and used especially as refrigerants, in the production of foam plastics, and in aerosols. If the depletion of the ozone layer and the creation of 'ozone holes' were to continue, the increased impact of ultra-violet rays could affect not only the animal food chain, but also human health; and whereas cause and effect cannot be conclusively proved there is sufficient reason to justify a total and world-wide ban on them. CFCs also have an effect on global warming: but their long-term impact is uncertain.

As a result of initiatives in this direction, the Vienna Convention for the protection of the Ozone Layer was signed in 1985, followed by the 1987 Montreal Protocol on Substances that Deplete the Ozone Layer, to which there are now sixty signatories. Incremental costs relating to the phasing out of CFCs can be funded in developing country signatories from the Montreal Fund which was established by the Montreal Protocol. The European Community and other major industrialised countries have agreed to forbid the manufacture and use of CFCs.

# (2)  GLOBAL WARMING AND THE GREENHOUSE EFFECT

Whereas change is the essence of the earth's climate – whether in cycles of decades, centuries or millennia, it remains a fact that the rapidly increasing use of fossil fuels could result in unexpected and dangerous consequences; resulting products such as carbon dioxide, methane and nitrous oxide are known to trap heat and create a 'greenhouse' effect. There is always the possibility that global warming might trigger off unexpected and potentially disastrous changes, but its main impact would be to alter the regional emphasis of the world's climate and consequently the agriculture – with unknown social and political consequences – and gradually raise the level of the seas and influence ocean currents and marine life.

The major cause of global warming is judged to be the use of fossil fuels – oil, lignite, coal, and wood – mainly in industry, transport and the generation of electricity, but also for domestic purposes; but reservations in respect of the use of nuclear fuels prevents serious reduction of the output of carbon dioxide. Funds for the reduction in growth of global warming gases are to be made available by donor countries through the Global Environment Facility, a joint organisation of the World Bank, the United Nations Development Programme and the United Nations Environmental Programme.

## (3) BIODIVERSITY

The relatively recent discovery of DNA has opened up the field of genetic engineering, with its prospects of worldwide benefits especially in medicine. Bio-technology, however, is dependent upon the preservation of biodiversity – the vast number of different forms of life existing on the planet – and the ability to have access to such sources. These two matters – preservation and access – more particularly the financial basis on which access is permitted were the subject of the Convention on Bio-Diversity signed at the 1992 Earth Summit in Rio de Janerio.

## (4) THE PRESERVATION OF FORESTS

The preservation of forests – particularly the rainforests – is seen as the major element in the maintenance of biodiversity, and their diminution or destruction would, in addition, undoubtedly result in a change of influence of the world's climate.

The origins of the 1992 United Nations Conference on Environment and Development, the 'Earth Summit', are to be found in an instruction from the Secretary General to create a World Commission on

'how the human species could make economic
progress within nature's strict laws'.

It would be hard to find words that more precisely sum up the essence of the problem that diplomats have to face. The Earth Summit produced a non-binding Earth Charter and Agenda 21 with excellent intentions, but supreme diplomatic skills will be necessary if the imperative of economic progress is to be reconciled with the inflexibility of nature's strict laws.

*Appendix E*

# GLOSSARY OF DIPLOMATIC, CONSULAR, LEGAL AND ECONOMIC TERMS

*above the line payments and receipts*, payments and receipts contained in that part of the government's budget dealing with expenditure to be met out of revenue raised mainly from taxation

*abrogate*, to annul, revoke (e.g. a treaty)

*ad hominem*, on an individual basis

*ad valorem tax*, a duty imposed on goods in proportion to their value, i.e. a duty expressed as a percentage, and not a specific amount

*ad interim*, temporary; during the intervening period of time

*ad referendum*, subject to confirmation

*amortisation*, the gradual repayment of a debt by means of a sinking fund

*annexation*, the acquisition by a state of additional territory

*appellation d'origine*, the name given to a commodity indicating its place of origin

*arbitration*, the judgment of a dispute by an agreed third party, the matter to be resolved on the basis of international law, and the decision to be binding on the parties concerned

*autarky*, self-sufficiency (e.g. national economic self-sufficiency)

*autocracy*, government or control by a single person

*balance of payments*, the relation between the payments of all kinds made from one country to the rest of the world and its receipts from all other countries

*balance of trade*, the relationship between a country's merchandise imports ('visible imports') and its merchandise exports ('visible exports'). It excludes current payments and receipts for services and capital account items

*bank rate*, the minimum rate at which a central bank will discount first-class bills

*basket*, a jargon term, first popularised at the meetings of the Conference on Security and Cooperation in Europe, to refer to

175

a grouping of items or subjects. In financial circles it refers to a collection of different currencies

*becquerel*, unit of measurement of radioactivity

*belligerency*, a term of legal significance to describe a particular state of aggression

*below the line payments and receipts*, payments and receipts contained in that part of the government's budget dealing with capital items

*Benelux*, customs union established between Belgium, the Netherlands and Luxembourg

*bill of exchange*, an order for the making of payment, mainly used in international trade. A term bill may not be payable until, say, ninety days after acceptance; a sight bill is payable upon acceptance

*bill of lading*, a document of title to goods received for shipment

*bonded warehouse*, warehouse in which dutiable articles may be stored without payment of duty until they are withdrawn

*Bourse*, the Paris Stock Exchange and money market; term widely used for similar institutions in other countries

*Boycott*, the refusal to do business with a state (or person)

*broker*, an intermediary between two or more persons engaged in a business transaction

*budget*, an estimate of national revenue and expenditure for the ensuing fiscal year

*buffer state*, one situated between more powerful neighbours which relies for its security largely on the fact that no one neighbouring state is prepared to let it be occupied by a third state

*bullion*, gold and silver in bulk

*buyers' market*, a market in which producers, suppliers and dealers experience difficulty in selling the goods which are available

*capital expenditure*, expenditure of a non-recurrent nature resulting in the acquisition of assets

*capital intensive*, forms of production in which there is a considerable use of capital equipment per person employed relative to the labour employed

*capital market*, a market comprising institutions which deal in the purchase and sale of securities

*cartel*, a central selling organisation which assigns to each of its members a specific share in the total output of a commodity

*casus belli*, an action justifying a declaration of war

*caveat*, a request for action to be deferred, a proviso

*central bank*, a bank which in any country is (a) banker to the government, (b) banker to the commercial banks and (c) implements the currency and credit policy of the country

*certificate of origin*, a declaration by an exporter or by a chamber of commerce stating the country of origin of goods shipped *chargé d'affaires ad interim*, the member of the diplomatic staff of a mission (save in exceptional cases) who acts as head of mission during the latter's absence or indisposition, or in the interval between appointments

*chargé d'affaires en titre*, the head of a diplomatic mission accredited to a Minister for Foreign Affairs

*cheap money*, a description applied to money when the bank rate is low

*c.i.f.*, cost, insurance and freight, i.e. a quoted price for goods shipped c.i.f. includes all charges up to the point where the goods are deposited on board ship (f.o.b.) and also the cost of their insurance and freight

*COCOM*, an international agreement between the NATO countries (except Ireland) and Australia and Japan to limit the export of agreed items in the fields of:

(i) armaments; (ii) nuclear equipment; and (iii) sensitive technologies

*cold war*, a term used to denote the *degree* of hostility between states when their foreign policy interests clash one with another: the final stage in the spectrum of aggression conducted by non-military means

*commission (consular)*, a commission of appointment

*concordat*, an agreement concluded between a state and the Holy See

*confrontation*, a situation (usually between two states) which threatens to develop into a physical conflict in which neither party shows a willingness to give way

*consular invoice*, an invoice certified by the consul of an overseas country relating to goods shipped to that country

*consumer goods*, products in the actual form in which they will reach domestic consumers

*Contadora Group*, consisting of Colombia, Mexico, Panama and Venezuela, and joined in 1985 by a Support Group consisting of Argentina, Brazil, Paraguay and Peru. Their objective is to seek peace, respect for frontiers, democracy, human rights and arms reduction in Central America through negotiation

*contract*, an agreement, either oral or in writing, whereby two or more parties mutually undertake specific commitments

*convertibility*, the freedom to exchange any currency for another currency at the ruling rate of exchange

*conveyance*, legal description for the transfer of property from a seller to a buyer

*countervailing duty*, a tax levied on imports to counteract an unfair advantage, especially government subsidies and dumping, and to protect a domestic industry *coup d'état*, unlawful seizure of control of a government by persons (often military) occupying positions of authority

*current expenditure*, expenditure recurrent in nature and not resulting in the acquisition of assets

*customs cooperation council nomenclature*, the internationally accepted standardised system of describing goods for customs purposes (successor to the Brussels Tariff Nomenclature)

*customs duties*, duties levied on goods entering one state or region from another

*customs union*, a grouping of states or regions to form a single customs territory: tariffs and other trade restrictions between the member states or countries are abolished, and the union maintains a common external tariff against other countries

*de facto* (recognition) as a matter of fact

*deficit financing*, the financing of a budget deficit by a government by means of borrowing in the market or from the central bank

*deflation*, a situation in which prices and money incomes are falling, accompanied by an increase in the value of the monetary unit

*de jure* (recognition) in accordance with international law

*delegate*, a person to whom responsibility to act (usually to a specified extent) has been delegated (e.g. by a government)

*démarche*, an initiative or approach by a government, often based on a fresh policy following an unsatisfactory situation

*demurrage*, delay; caused to shipping, goods, etc., and the payment of fees or compensation as a result

*debt-service ratio*, the relationship between a country's foreign debt repayments (interest and capital) and its export earnings, expressed in percentage terms

*derogation*, the temporary suspension of the enforcement of a provision (EC)

*de rigeur*, obligatory

*détente*, relaxation of tension

*devaluation*, the determination of a new and lower (i.e. fewer units of foreign currency per unit of home currency) fixed exchange rate for a currency

*diplomatic asylum*, political asylum granted in the premises of a diplomatic mission or other such premises entitled to inviolability

*diplomatic conference*, as for Plenipotentiary Conference (q.v.)

*disinflation*, the removal of inflationary pressure from the economy in order to maintain the value of the monetary unit

*domino theory*, the theory that in a certain set of circumstances the fall of a government or state will bring about the downfall of a neighbouring government or state which, in falling, will set in train a succession of similar downfalls (a similar concept is 'to fall like a house of cards') *double taxation agreement*, an agreement to prevent the same income being taxed twice

*drawback*, the repayment of the import duty an exporter has had to pay on foreign materials or components contained in the goods he exports

*dumping*, the sale of goods in foreign markets at less than their net cost in the domestic market. The term 'non-commercial competition' is similarly applied to services, e.g. shipping

*economic growth*, the growth per head of the population in the production of goods and services of all kinds available to meet demand

*ecu*, the unit of currency of the European Community, based on the weighted value of the currencies of all the member countries with the exception of Greece. It is the world's fourth most important bond issue currency denomination, after the dollar, the deutschmark and sterling

*en clair*, in clear (as opposed to being in code or in cipher)

*en marge*, incidentally: used in the sense of discussions held during the course of a meeting but not necessarily related to the topic of the meeting

*en poste*, having assumed duties at the authorised (diplomatic or consular) post

*en principe* (English), as a matter of principle

*en principe* (French), generally speaking, as a rule

*entrepôt*, a place where merchandise is collected and stored for subsequent distribution.

*entrepreneur*, a person who undertakes trading transactions on his own account

*escalate*, to accelerate and increase in intensity or magnitude

*euro-dollar(s)*, private dollar balances held in European commercial banks

*exchange rate parity*, the fixed rate of exchange between one currency and another

*excise duties*, duties or taxes imposed on goods produced and distributed within a country

*ex officio*, by virtue of a specific post or office. Appointments to committees may be *ex officio*, i.e. the holder of a particular post is appointed for so long as he holds the post: the appointment does not relate to him personally

*explanations of vote*, verbal statement explaining why a vote has been cast in a particular way

*export duties*, duties or taxes imposed on goods exported from a country

*exposé*, revelation in public of a matter hitherto secret

*extra-territorial*, outside the jurisdiction of a territory *fait accompli*, an act that has been committed and is therefore no longer open to discussion

*f.a.s.*, free alongside (see f.o.b.,): a quoted price for goods shipped which includes all payments and charges up to the point of the goods being deposited on the quay alongside the ship

*fast track*, a procedure adopted by the American Congress whereby they agree to accept or reject (but not amend) an agreement within ninety working days

*faux pas*, a blunder (literally a false step)

*feasibility study*, the study of a proposed project in its technical and economic aspects to ascertain the possibility of commercial exploitation

*fiduciary issue*, that portion of the bank note issue which is not backed by gold

*fiscal policy*, the policy adopted by a government for raising revenue to meet expenditure and for influencing the level of business activity

*flag of convenience*, the flag of a state whose laws relating to shipping are less onerous on shipowners than other states: vessels registered in such a state fly its flag, and their crews are subject to its laws

*floating debt*, that part of the national debt which involves short-term borrowing

*floating exchange rate*, an exchange rate of any currency free to float to any level which supply and demand may determine

*f.o.b.*, free on board (see f.a.s. for elucidation)

*force majeure*, unavoidable and usually unforeseen circumstances

*free port*, an enclosed policed area in an airport, seaport or other locality into which goods may be imported and processed or manufactured without payment of customs duty of the country in which it is situated provided that they are re-exported subsequently to a third country

*free trade*, trade which is unimpeded by tariffs, import and export quotas and other devices which obstruct the free movement of goods and services between countries

*free trade area*, a grouping of states or regions within which customs duties and other barriers to trade are removed, but which has no common external tariff

*funding*, the conversion of short-term debts into long-term debts

*futures market*, a market in which goods are sold for delivery at some future date

*generalised system of preferences*, arrangement whereby the exports of developing countries are admitted to the industrialised countries duty-free up to a certain level, or at reduced rates, on a non-reciprocal basis *giro system*, a mechanism for the transfer of payments operated by the post office

*glasnost*, openness (Russian)

*gold standard*, a monetary system in which each unit of currency is worth a fixed amount of gold. The rules of a gold standard are:

    (a) all paper currency must be convertible at its face value into gold;

    (b) there must be no restrictions on the import or export of gold;

    (c) a gold reserve must be maintained, fully sufficient to meet all demands made upon it.

*gross domestic product*, the value of goods and services produced within the State

*gross national product*, gross domestic product plus net income from interest, profit and dividends derived from assets abroad

*group of 77*, group of developing countries, now over 130 in number (originally formed at UNCTAD I)

*Group of Seven*, major industrialised countries: Canada, France, Germany, Italy, Japan, United Kingdom, United States of America

*Group of Ten*, the countries with a controlling majority in the IMF (currently eleven in number)

*group of fifteen* (G15), association of developing countries with mutual economic interests *vis-à-vis* the G7

*group of twenty*, committee of the ten controlling members of the IMF and ten members of developing countries

*Holy See*, the legal and symbolic personification of the Roman Catholic Church of which the Pope is Supreme Pontiff. He is also Sovereign Pontiff of the State of Vatican City

*hot money*, money which is transferred between countries in order to benefit from advantageous rates of interest or in anticipation of a change in the parity of a currency

*hot pursuit*, a legal doctrine of nautical application permitting the apprehension of vessels which are believed to have committed an offence within a state's territorial waters, and then have escaped on to the seas. The term is also used to attempt to justify similar actions in respect of persons escaping from one state to another by land

*impasse*, a situation of immobility or stalemate, in which no party involved can make a move

*incognito*, without revealing one's identity

*inflation*, a condition in which the volume of purchasing power is constantly running ahead of the output of goods and services, with the result that as incomes and prices rise the value of money falls

181

*infrastructure*, services regarded as essential for the creation of a modern economy, e.g. power, transport, housing, education and health services

*innocent passage*, the right of any sea-going vessel of any state to pass through the territorial waters of another state provided that this is done innocently, and to stop and anchor but only in accordance with navigational requirements, *force majeure* or distress. Certain states demand prior notification or approval for warships. Submarines must travel on the surface and show their flag

*inter alia*, among other things

*invisible earnings*, in national accounting, receipts for services rendered (e.g. shipping, banking, insurance tourism)

*junta*, a committee or a group of people working together; usually used to refer to a revolutionary government consisting of members of a group (e.g. the army)

*jus sanguinis* (nationality), based on blood relationship

*jus soli* (nationality), based on the place of birth

*labour-intensive*, form of production in which there is a considerable use of labour in relation to the amount of capital equipment per unit of output

*laissez-faire*, a policy of non-interference by the state in economic affairs

*laissez-passer*, a permit to travel or to enter a particular area

*lapsus linguae*, a slip of the tongue – a spoken error (Latin)

*legal tender*, money which a person is obliged by law to accept in payment of a debt

*liquid assets*, assets either in the form of money, or which can be quickly converted into money

*Lombard rate*, the rate at which a Central Bank makes loans to commercial banks against eligible securities (e.g. government bonds)

*memorandum of association*, a document specifying the aims and objects of a commercial company

*merchant banks*, banks whose business consists mainly of the accepting of commercial bills and the financing of trade

*mixed economy*, an economy in which resources are allocated partly through the decisions of private individuals and privately-owned business enterprises, and partly through the decisions of the government and state-owned enterprises: the two sectors are respectively known as the private and public sectors

*modus vivendi*, an arrangement which enables all concerned to carry on their activities in spite of disagreements, or while a disagreement is being resolved

*most-favoured-nation clause*, a clause which may be included in a commercial treaty between two nations that they will mutually grant to each other any favourable treatment which either may accord to a third nation in respect of customs duties

*motions for division*, provide for separate voting on separate sections of a resolution

*multi-fibre arrangement*, an agreement between 41 developed and developing countries to protect the textile industries of the former by limiting imports from the latter

*national debt*, the debts of a government, both internal and external

*national income*, a measure of the money value of the goods and services becoming available to a nation from economic activity during a prescribed period, usually a year

*nautical mile*, a distance of 2,025 yards or 1,852 metres, equal to one minute of the earth's measurement

*non-aligned movement*, group of 177 states originally uncommitted in the Cold War; now concerned with a new world order and economic development

*notarial acts*, the acts of an official (e.g. a consular officer) who attests and certifies documents

*oligarchy*, rule by a very small section of a state or community

*oligopoly*, a market structure in which only a few firms compete

*ordre du jour*, agenda

*package deal*, an agreement incorporating a variety of diverse elements

*pacta sunt servanda*, the legal doctrine that a treaty constitutes a contract between the parties, and that its conditions are binding and must be observed

*pari passu*, in step; by equal stages

*Paris club*, association of major creditor states concerned with re-negotiating and, where appropriate, re-scheduling official foreign debts

*plenipotentiary conference*, a conference meeting for the purpose of drawing up or revising an international instrument at which delegates have full powers

*post mortem*, an analysis or enquiry into an event, primarily to see what lessons for the future can be learnt from it (Latin: 'after the death')

*Pressler amendment*, policy of limiting US aid to non-nuclear states

*prima facie*, on the basis of the evidence immediately available

*private sector*, the private sector of the economy is the combination of elements in the economy which are not organs or agencies of central or local government and therefore includes the company sector and the personal sector

*procedural motion*, relates to the conduct of a meeting and must immediately be put to the vote by the presiding officer

*procès-verbale*, the minutes of a meeting

*producer goods*, goods made for the purpose of producing consumer goods, e.g. machinery of all kinds

*productivity*, the efficiency with which productive resources, i.e. labour, capital and land, are used, usually expressed as output per unit of input

*pronunciamiento*, a proclamation or manifesto, usually associated with the revolutionary takeover of a government

*protocol* (i) formal diplomatic behaviour; (ii) an international agreement, usually supplementary to a major treaty

*protocol of signature*, an addendum to a treaty usually recording clarifications or reservations

*proviso*, an exception

*public sector*, the public sector of the economy usually denotes the combination of the central government, the local authorities, the nationalised industries and other public corporations.

*purchasing power parity*, the exchange rate between two currencies that would result in equal purchasing power in the currency areas concerned

*quid pro quo*, something given in return for something else; a consideration

*quiproquo* (French), a misunderstanding; at cross-purposes

*rapporteur*, the person who makes a summary of e.g. the proceedings of a conference

*rapprochement*, a renewal of improved relations between states

*real terms*, sums of money expressed in 'real terms' take account of the changing value of money; the change is usually related to a particular 'base year'

*rebus sic stantibus*, the legal doctrine which asserts that if the conditions under which a treaty was concluded have fundamentally altered, then the treaty may be said to be no longer binding

*shipping conference*, an association of shipowners, the main purpose of which is to fix rates to be charged and to allocate ports of call

*sine qua non*, an essential, something without which something else would not be possible

*sinking fund*, a fund built up by periodic instalments in order to accumulate a certain sum at a given date for some specific purpose

*social dumping*, in a free trade or low-tariff area, the transfer of industry or other sources of employment from a member-country where the levels of social costs and labour legislation are high to a member-country where they are low

*special drawing rights*, a system of international reserve assets created by the International Monetary Fund

*specific tariff*, a tariff reckoned in terms of a specific amount of money for each unit of the commodity concerned (e.g. 30 cents per kg) *spot market*, a market in which goods are sold for immediate delivery

*status quo*, the existing situation

*suaviter in modo, fortiter in re*, firm in purpose, courteous in manner

*tariff*, a duty or tax charged by a country on its imports from other countries; a customs duty

*territorial asylum*, political asylum granted by a state to an alien in its territory

*trade creation*, in a Common Market or Free Trade Area the replacement of high-cost imported goods by low-cost articles produced within the area (e.g. benefiting from the economies of scale)

*trade deflection*, in a Free Trade Area the importation of goods into a member country with a low external tariff for consumption in another with a high external tariff in an attempt to pay the minimum duty

*trade diversion*, in a Common Market or Free Trade Area the substitution of cheap imported goods by more costly articles produced within the area

*trade gap*, the difference between the value of imports c.i.f., and exports (and re-exports) f.o.b.

*trademark*, the brand name or other device used to relate a commodity to the particular firm owning, producing or distributing it

*tranche*, literally a slice or segment: term used by the IMF referring to a credit granted to a member state. This is allocated in four tranches, each being dependent upon the acceptance by the member country of increasing degrees of financial stringency

*ultimatum*, final demand

*ultra vires*, not within the law

*unit of account*, in the European Community, the monetary unit used for fixing the price of agricultural produce, etc.

*veto*, a negative vote

*volte face*, an abrupt and complete reversal of previous policy

*visible exports*, exports which consist of tangible goods such as plant and machinery, consumer goods, etc.

# NUCLEAR NON-PROLIFERATION

A concomitant of the Cold War was the development and proliferation of nuclear armaments, both on the part of the major
antagonists and of various non-aligned states. The end of the
Cold War has presented the world community of states with the
opportunity to reduce and eventually eliminate nuclear armaments: failing which they will inevitably continue the process of
proliferation as every regional 'superpower' seeks either to extend
its hegemony or to match the nuclear capability of a potential rival
or aggressor.

The Treaty on the Non-Proliferation of Nuclear Weapons (NPT)
came into force in March 1970, and its basic aims are to prevent
the further spread of nuclear weapons; to foster peaceful nuclear
cooperation under safeguards, and to encourage negotiations to end
competitive development of nuclear weapons with a view to their
eventual elimination.

Under the terms of the Treaty, nuclear-weapon states agree not
to assist non-nuclear-weapon states to acquire nuclear explosive
devices; and the latter agree not to manufacture or otherwise
acquire such devices. Provision is made for the International Atomic
Energy Agency to apply safeguards, including inspection in respect
of nuclear material used in the peaceful programmes of non-nuclear
weapon states which are parties to the treaty. The dangers of nuclear
proliferation, not least of nuclear technology and know-how, have
increased considerably since the break-up of the Soviet Union, and
the member states of the European Community made recognition
of those members of the Commonwealth of Independent States on
whose territory nuclear weapons were stationed, conditional on their
adherence to the treaty as non-nuclear weapon states.

There are 140 parties to the treaty, including the existing nuclear
powers (with the exception of North Korea) who have also agreed
to the Missile Technology Control Regime.

Review Conferences have been held every five years in accordance with the treaty, and in 1995 when the treaty comes to the end of its twenty-five-year duration, the contracting parties will be required to reconsider the role of nuclear armaments in the context of the evolution of a New World Order.

# INDEX

*Index*

Head of Mission (*see also* Diplomatic
agent *and* Foreign Affairs)
absence of, 8–10, 23
accreditation and appointment, 4–7
defined, 1–7, 14–18
precedence, 15, 29, 31
recall or withdrawal, 8, 9–10, 26–7
relations with own or host ministry,
12–15, 17–18, 24–7, 32–5, 39–40
High Commissioners, 4
Holy See, 177, 181
representatives, 4, 15, 29–30
Hospitality *see* Entertaining
Human Rights, 93–5

Identity cards, 49
Immunities *see* Privileges
Indian Ocean Commission, 110
Information section, 12, 21–2
Intergovernmental Maritime
Organisation (IMO), 86–7
International Atomic Energy Agency
(IAEA), 77
International Bank for Reconstruction
and Development (IBRD), 79–85
International Civil Aviation
Organisation (ICAO), 85
International Court of Justice (ICJ), 67,
74–5, 126
International Development Association
(IDA) (*see also* IBRD), 79–80
International Finance Corporation
(IFC), 79–80
International Labour Organisation
(ILO), 77, 143
International Law *see* Law, International
International Law Commission (ILC),
92–3
International Monetary Fund and
Institute (IMF), 80–5, 143, 184
International Research and Training
Institute for the Advancement of
Women (INSTRAW), 95
International Telecommunications
Union (ITU), 86
Islam, 171
Islamic Conference Organisations, 110

Jurisdiction, extent of state, 136–7

Kaufmann, Johan, Conference
Diplomacy, 137

Latin American Economic
Organisations, 111–12

Latin American Integration Association
(LAIA *or* ALADI), 111
Law, International (*see also* Court of
Justice), 11–12, 74–5, 92–3, 121–38
League of Arab States, 97
Legation, 4
Letters (*see also* Diplomatic
correspondence *and* Notes)
exchange of, 123
of Credence, 4–5, 24–6
of intent, 125
of introduction, 5
of recall, 26
rejection of, 35
List, Consular and Diplomatic, 31–2, 49

Mano River Union (MRU), 119
Mercosur, 112
Ministers and Ministries of Foreign
Affairs *see* Foreign Affairs
Mourning, official, 36, 39–40

Nationality, 137–8
of consular officials, 54–5
of members of diplomatic mission, 6,
20
North American Free Trade
Agreement, 113
North Atlantic Treaty Organisation
(NATO), 112–13
Note (*see also* Diplomatic
correspondence), 33–5
*Note, verbale*, 33
Nuclear non-proliferation, 186–7

Organisation for Economic Cooperation
and Development (OECD), 113–14
Organisation for the Development of
the Senegal River (OMVS), 119
Organisation of African Unity (OAU),
114–15
Organisation of American States
(OAS), 115
Organisation of Eastern Caribbean
States (OECS), 99–100
Organisation of the Petroleum
Exporting Countries (OPEC), 116

Pact (*see also* Agreement, Convention,
Declaration *and* Treaty)
Cairo (1945), 97
Papal Nuncio *see* Holy See
Paris Club, 183
Passport (*see also* Visa), 53
diplomatic, 49

190